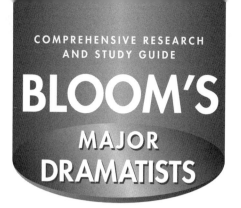

COMPREHENSIVE RESEARCH
AND STUDY GUIDE

BLOOM'S
MAJOR
DRAMATISTS

Bertolt
Brecht

EDITED AND WITH AN
INTRODUCTION BY HAROLD BLOOM

BLOOM'S MAJOR DRAMATISTS

Aeschylus

Anton Chekhov

Aristophanes

Berthold Brecht

Euripides

Henrik Ibsen

Ben Johnson

Christopher Marlowe

Arthur Miller

Eugene O'Neill

Shakespeare's Comedies

Shakespeare's Histories

Shakespeare's Romances

Shakespeare's Tragedies

George Bernard Shaw

Neil Simon

Sophocles

Tennessee Williams

August Wilson

BLOOM'S MAJOR NOVELISTS

Jane Austen

The Brontës

Willa Cather

Stephen Crane

Charles Dickens

Fyodor Dostoevsky

William Faulkner

F. Scott Fitzgerald

Thomas Hardy

Nathaniel Hawthorne

Ernest Hemingway

Henry James

James Joyce

D. H. Lawrence

Toni Morrison

John Steinbeck

Stendhal

Leo Tolstoy

Mark Twain

Alice Walker

Edith Wharton

Virginia Woolf

BLOOM'S MAJOR WORLD POETS

Geoffrey Chaucer

Emily Dickinson

John Donne

T. S. Eliot

Robert Frost

Langston Hughes

John Milton

Edgar Allan Poe

Shakespeare's Poems & Sonnets

Alfred, Lord Tennyson

Walt Whitman

William Wordsworth

BLOOM'S MAJOR SHORT STORY WRITERS

William Faulkner

F. Scott Fitzgerald

Ernest Hemingway

O. Henry

James Joyce

Herman Melville

Flannery O'Connor

Edgar Allan Poe

J. D. Salinger

John Steinbeck

Mark Twain

Eudora Welty

COMPREHENSIVE RESEARCH
AND STUDY GUIDE

BLOOM'S
MAJOR
DRAMATISTS

*Bertolt
Brecht*

EDITED AND WITH AN INTRODUCTION
BY HAROLD BLOOM

© 2002 by Chelsea House Publishers, a subsidiary of
Haights Cross Communications.

Introduction © 2002 by Harold Bloom.

Printed and bound in the United States of America.

First Printing
1 3 5 7 9 8 6 4 2

Library of Congress Cataloging-in-Publication Data
applied for

ISBN 0–7910–6363–1

Chelsea House Publishers
1974 Sproul Road, Suite 400
Broomall, PA 19008-0914

The Chelsea House World Wide Web address is
http://www.chelseahouse.com

Series Editor: Matt Uhler

Contributing Editor: Martina Kolb

Produced by Publisher's Services, Santa Barbara, California

Contents

User's Guide

This volume is designed to present biographical, critical, and bibliographical information on the author's best-known or most important works. Following Harold Bloom's editor's note and introduction is a detailed biography of the author, discussing major life events and important literary accomplishments. A plot summary of each play follows, tracing significant themes, patterns, and motifs in the work.

A selection of critical extracts, derived from previously published material from leading critics, analyzes aspects of each play. The extracts consist of statements from the author, if available, early reviews of the work, and later evaluations up to the present. A bibliography of the author's writings (including a complete list of all works written, cowritten, edited, and translated), a list of additional books and articles on the author and his or her work, and an index of themes and ideas in the author's writings conclude the volume.

〜

Harold Bloom is Sterling Professor of the Humanities at Yale University and Henry W. and Albert A. Berg Professor of English at the New York University Graduate School. He is the author of over 20 books, including *Shelley's Mythmaking* (1959), *The Visionary Company* (1961), *Blake's Apocalypse* (1963), *Yeats* (1970), *A Map of Misreading* (1975), *Kabbalah and Criticism* (1975), *Agon: Toward a Theory of Revisionism* (1982), *The American Religion* (1992), *The Western Canon* (1994), and *Omens of Millennium: The Gnosis of Angels, Dreams, and Resurrection* (1996). *The Anxiety of Influence* (1973) sets forth Professor Bloom's provocative theory of the literary relationships between the great writers and their predecessors. His most recent books include *Shakespeare: The Invention of the Human*, a 1998 National Book Award finalist, and *How to Read and Why*, which was published in 2000.

Professor Bloom earned his Ph.D. from Yale University in 1955 and has served on the Yale faculty since then. He is a 1985 MacArthur Foundation Award recipient, served as the Charles Eliot Norton Professor of Poetry at Harvard University in 1987–88, and has received honorary degrees from the universities of Rome and Bologna. In 1999, Professor Bloom received the prestigious American Academy of Arts and Letters Gold Medal for Criticism.

Currently, Harold Bloom is the editor of numerous Chelsea House volumes of literary criticism, including the series BLOOM'S NOTES, BLOOM'S MAJOR DRAMATISTS, BLOOM'S MAJOR NOVELISTS, MAJOR LITERARY CHARACTERS, MODERN CRITICAL VIEWS, MODERN CRITICAL INTERPRETATIONS, and WOMEN WRITERS OF ENGLISH AND THEIR WORKS.

Editor's Note

My Introduction considers something of the extent to which the poet-dramatist "Brecht" was a fiction, since the largest part of Brecht's work was composed by women who were in love with him.

On *The Threepenny Opera,* Frederic Ewen celebrates the work's ironical and parodistic tonalities, while Willy Haas evokes the historical moment, and Karl H. Schoeps compares the adaptation to John Gay's original. To Stephen McNeff, the genre is *montage.*

On *Mother Courage,* Franz N. Mennemeier salutes the ballad style, while Roland Barthes, studying photographs of a performance, praises Brechtian estrangement or alienation, and Charles R. Lyons appreciates the play's sense that war is a business, like any other. To Robert Leach, the Brechtian dialectic refuses resolution, after which Robert Potter discusses his American revision of *Mother Courage.*

On *The Good Woman of Sezuan,* Eric Bentley discusses problems of translation, while John Fuegi centers on the problematics of good and evil, and Sieglinde Lug uncovers the play's potential feminism. To Ronald Speirs, *The Good Woman* is a success of parable, after which Elizabeth Wright also offers a feminist interpretation.

On *Galileo,* Günter Rohrmoser compares the three versions, while M. A. Cohen sees the play as history in the Elizabethan sense, and Betty N. Weber interprets the hero as a version of Leon Trotsky. To Guy Stern, Brecht's own exile is the hidden theme, after which Doc Rossi sees *Hamlet* as Brecht's paradigm.

On *The Caucasian Chalk Circle,* Ronald Gray praises the play's detachment, while Maria P. Alter also explores the use of the alienation technique, and Helen M. Whall asks us to see a Brechtian salvation of pastoral from mere nostalgia. Finally, to Maria Shevtsova, a European perspective reveals the play's concern with the war between Russia and Germany.

Introduction

HAROLD BLOOM

"Bertolt Brecht," as we continue to learn, was a brand name, applied by Bert Brecht, a survivor, to the writing of some of the women he made love to and exploited: Elisabeth Hauptmann, Margarete Steffin, and Ruth Berlau. Brecht himself was remarkably reluctant to write plays, poems, or stories entirely on his own. Of the five plays studied in this volume, Hauptmann composed most of *The Threepenny Opera* (80 to 90 percent) and Steffin the larger part of *Mother Courage and Her Children, Galileo, The Good Woman of Sezuan,* and *The Caucasian Chalk Circle.* Berlau wrote part of *The Good Woman of Sezuan,* so this book actually should be called *Bloom's Dramatists: Elisabeth Hauptmann, Margarete Steffin, Ruth Berlau, and Bert Brecht,* but a brand name is a brand name, as I cheerfully acknowledge.

Marxist anti-individualism, served with French sauces, is now nearly dominant in the university, and affects the media and entertainment industries. Doubtless, Brecht was acting on his principles, though one can wince at his sermons on "goodness," while enjoying his famous maxims: "First comes eating, then comes morality" and "For this life no person is bad enough." His early poem, "Concerning Poor B.B.," has a delicious passage where he reclines, amidst a pair of women, whom he assures: "In me you behold a man upon whom absolutely you can't rely." Whether Hauptmann wrote some, or even all, of *this* poem is a nice question.

At what point does anti-individualism become plain theft? As a lifelong anti-Nazi, Brecht had his heroic aspect. Unfortunately, he defended Stalin endlessly, slyly blind even to the disappearance of old friends into the gulag. The truth appears to be that Marxism had nothing to do with Brecht's lifelong exploitation of his many women. He was a timeless womanizer and cad, greatly gifted in the mysteries by which women of genius are caught and held.

All this is merely preamble to the rest of this Introduction, where the brand name "Brecht" is employed, even though the dramatist's name ought to be Hauptmann, or Steffin, or Steffin and Berlau. As research more fully establishes actual authorship, Hauptmann and

Steffin, in particular, will replace Brecht, and will be seen as major dramatists in the German language. But it is awkward to keep putting "Brecht" into quotation marks, so I will just say Brecht, while urging the reader to keep in mind that Brecht was not Brecht.

Since Brecht may have composed no more than a tenth of *The Threepenny Opera,* perhaps we ought to start calling it Hauptmann/Brecht/Weill anyway. Even that is inaccurate, since Brecht usurped Karl Kammer's translations of poems by François Villon, without changing a word, and of course without acknowledgment, so we actually have *The Threepenny Opera* (1928) by Hauptmann/Brecht/Weill/Kammer. John Gay and Villon mix well, Brecht cleverly saw. As a poet, Brecht owed something to Heine, a touch to Villon and Rimbaud, but most to Elisabeth Hauptmann, and then to Margarete Steffin, after her.

The Threepenny Opera has taken the place of *The Beggar's Opera,* its archetype, though I still prefer John Gay's work, whether as reading or in performance. "The Ballad of Mac the Knife," as sung and trumpeted by Louis Armstrong, remains the largest intrusion of Brecht and Company into popular American consciousness.

Tony Kushner, a generous and gifted Marxist idealizer, tells us that: "The smallest divisible human unit is two people, not one; one is a fiction." Alas, the experience of a lifetime teaches me otherwise: two is a fiction. Bert Brecht, whatever he said he believed, pragmatically demonstrated that, except for Bert, everyone else was a staged fiction.

The plays, when well directed and performed, are more impressive than they are on the page. Reading Brecht and Company is, for me, a mixed aesthetic experience, because much of the cynicism is dated, the ideology is glaring, and the theories of alienation and of epic theater are all too relevant to the plays. Are there any personalities involved, let alone characters? The flight from pathos is brilliantly complete: why should we care? Didactic literature, Christian or Marxist, is moralism, not literature. Eloquence abides in Brecht and Company, and there are a wealth of dramatic effects, but to compare *Galileo* to *Hamlet* is an absurdity.

Eric Bentley, a dramatic critic to whom I defer, maintains his long devotion to Brecht and Company, and so I have to assume that, as a critic, I am insensitive to parable as a dramatic form. Still, there are questions to put to the Brechtians. If Hamlet were the political drama that Brecht turned it into, could it be of perpetual relevance, so universal, free of all restrictions of time and place? I attended the *Life of Galileo* that Charles Laughton brought to Broadway in December 1947, and recall being stunned by Laughton's vehement presence, his extraordinary pathos, which seemed incongruous in the context of the more-or-less Brechtian play, which was so uneasy with its own Shakespeareanism that I emerged from the theater totally confused. Reading the play's various texts since, in German, does not enlighten me, more than a half-century later. Even *Coriolanus* defeated Brecht's attempt to empty it of pathos, but the *Hamlet*-haunted *Galileo* attempts to hollow out what is much larger than itself. The land that does not need a hero is yet to be found. Brecht and Company was a brave and original venture, but a final aesthetic judgment upon it would still be premature. ❀

Biography of
Bertolt Brecht

Poet, playwright and director Bertolt Brecht was one of the most significant writers of the 20th century. His international influence on the modern theater has frequently been compared to Franz Kafka's impact on the modern novel. Brecht's life and work were firmly anchored in the social, cultural, and political realities of the troubled first half of the 20th century.

Eugen Berthold Friedrich Brecht was born in Augsburg, southern Germany, in 1898. He was raised in Augsburg, and had his schooling there. Brecht was the son of a well-respected bourgeois family. During World War One he began his studies at the Munich University Medical School and in the Department of Philosophy, but one year later had to return to his home town to work as a medical orderly at the Augsburg military hospital. In 1919 Brecht had a son by Paula Banholzer; he died fighting on the Russian front in World War Two. Although Brecht took up his studies again, he never graduated, but instead seriously committed himself to the theater. In 1922 he received the Kleist prize for his play *Drums in the Night*—a Swabian-Bavarian regional play about the 1919 Spartacus revolt. In 1923 Brecht worked as theater critic and literary manager for the Munich theater (*Kammerspiele*), and then from 1924 to 1926 as dramaturge under Max Reinhardt for the Berlin theater (*Deutsches Theater*). From 1922 to 1926 Brecht was married to the Viennese opera-singer Marianne Zoff; they had a daughter, who under the name of Hanne Hiob was to become a successful actress.

In the late twenties, Bertolt Brecht began to familiarize himself with Erwin Piscator's political theater, as well as with Karl Marx's writings. From his Berlin studies of Marxism on, Brecht remained faithful to the socialism of both the Soviet Union and the later German Democratic Republic. As an immediate result of his intensive studies of Marxism, his strictly didactic plays (*Lehrstücke*) were mostly written in 1929 and 1930. Although often rashly characterized as dogmatic, Brecht's style is often less prescriptively pedagogical, but rather exposes the method of learning evident in the prologues and epilogues of the plays. These frames not only present a rupture to the event structure of the plays, but also descriptively contextualize the contents in a social, political and historical fashion. While clearly remaining didactic in nature, his later plays are equally strong in their culinary effect. His best works are fine examples of pleasurable learning in what Brecht labeled the *Epic Theater*.

In the late twenties, Brecht began to develop his idea of the epic theater. It is a theater that does not believe in an ideology of fate, and hence does not present a teleological plot line. Instead, it enumerates individual scenes as entities in their own right. Brecht formed this conception of the theater as a reaction to the theater and the opera of the 18th and 19th centuries. Epic theater does not set out to overwhelm the audience with emotions. It has no interest in capturing the spectators' hearts, but rather encourages them to engage rationally and think critically. A distance is willingly created between audience and stage, as well as between actor and role. If actors do not live their roles, but rather act them, it is easier for the spectator to avoid identification as well, and instead open up to the problem at stake, which asks for an intellectual input that affects could not solve.

Brecht was interested in activating the audience. He intended emotional detachment and favored techniques that provoke curiosity. He thought that rough language was most likely to stimulate dialectics of thought. Brecht's coinage *Verfremdungseffekt* or *V-Effekt* (effect of alienation, de-familiarization, or estrangement) figures most prominently in his theater and is *the* device to destroy illusions. It employs various techniques of breaking, distancing and debunking, most famously songs, slogans, banners, and narrators. And it most radically illustrates how Brecht's epic theater is anti-sentimental in its calculation of effects, for the V-effect is meant to avoid what traditional theater had been eager to promote: the spectators' identification and empathy with anything or anyone on stage. The V-effect thus prevents the so-called Aristotelian affects as well as a subsequent catharsis, and instead focuses on an intellectual dimension.

Brecht's radical rejection of empty pathos might partly have resulted from his middle-class upbringing, and partly from his growing skepticism toward Expressionism. Theatrical creations of anti-heroes such as Mac the Knife, *The Threepenny Opera*'s infamous rogue, or the sexy woman singing of alcohol and prostitution, became one of Brecht's strong suits. His matter-of-fact attitude was increasingly blended with a strict refusal of bourgeois identity, as well as with the formation of a revolutionary collective. He came to classify the middle-class world as an ideal instance of the grotesque, as a vexed form of complacent living, unable to advocate change. But what Brecht set out to convey was that change is both necessary and possible. Neither an ideology of fate, nor a Christian doctrine would allow for such change, so that Brecht felt the need to replace these ideologies by one of commitment.

One is well advised to take Brecht's own advice and not judge a book by its cover. Rumors on Brecht are legion. And rumor has it that a thriller covered by Marx's *Das Kapital* was found on Brecht's bedside table. Be that as it may. Brecht's entire oeuvre blends art and politics. It is critical and evokes criticism. Brecht was a cynical bohemian bogey of the middle classes, but also much more than a mere provocateur. He developed and dramatized his political knowledge in remarkable ways, and was an outspoken, radical opponent of the war, its nationalism and its capitalism. It is likely that he never was a member of the Communist Party, but nonetheless fifth on the National Socialist Party's black list in 1923. With Adolf Hitler's seizure of power in 1933 Brecht emigrated. First to Switzerland and then to Denmark, where his collaborators Elisabeth Hauptmann, Margarete Steffin and the Danish actress Ruth Berlau were of considerable assistance to him. In 1935 Brecht was expatriated. The defeat of the Spanish Republic and the 1938 Munich Agreement made danger even more explicit. He fled to Sweden in 1939, and after the German invasion in Denmark and Norway, Brecht escaped—via Finland and the USSR—to the United States in 1941.

Bertolt Brecht was an exile, and his art is an exile's art. His major works were written in or after his exile. He lived in the German exile community in Santa Monica until well after the war. In this Californian refuge he collaborated with Charles Chaplin and Charles Laughton. In 1947, Brecht moved to Zurich, Switzerland, and in 1949 settled in East Berlin. Together with his second wife Helene Weigel (with whom Brecht had a son and a daughter), and in marked contrast to the classical Weimar theater, Brecht and Weigel established the *Berlin Ensemble* in 1949, which secured world-wide recognition for the post-war Berlin stage. Stateless since the early thirties, Brecht and Weigel were granted Austrian citizenship in 1950.

In 1951 Brecht was awarded the National Prize, first class; in 1954 he became the vice-president of the Eastern German Academy of Arts; and in 1955 he received the Stalin prize in Moscow. From 1952 on, Brecht mostly worked in seclusion near a Buckow lake, while the East Berlin Chausseestraße was his official address from 1953 on. After his death in 1956, Weigel remained in charge of the *Berlin Ensemble,* and Elisabeth Hauptmann devoted herself to the editorial side of their many years of common effort in and for the theater. Brecht and his gifted as well as giving collaborators wrote more than thirty plays, about one hundred and fifty prose texts (not counting diaries or letters), roughly two thousand poems and songs, numerous fragments, and three novels. ❀

Plot Summary of
The Threepenny Opera
(Die Dreigroschenoper)

"Brecht & Co.'s" *The Threepenny Opera* has repeatedly been classified as a modern adaptation of John Gay's 18th-century *The Beggar's Opera*. Even though *The Threepenny Opera* significantly refashions Gay's work, Brecht's outline essentially remains Gay's. *The Beggar's Opera* itself is already a parody of the Baroque opera. Of course Brecht alters Gay's target. Gay ridiculed the English aristocracy, whereas Brecht presents the bourgeoisie as an entirely corrupt entity.

Brecht opposes two criminal parties in London at the turn of the century. A company that specializes in robbery, led by infamous MacHeath on the one hand, and on the other the begging specialists united in Jonathan Jeremiah Peachum's firm. The conflict is set in motion when Mackie secretly marries crook Peachum's daughter Polly in the presence of Tiger Brown. Peachum disapproves of the match and as a consequence has a strong desire for Mackie's arrest, so as to finally be able to remove him from the competitive criminal business scene. Although Mackie is about as unreliable as Brecht characterizes himself in his dubious autobiographical poem *Of Poor B.B.*, Polly means well with her groom and warns Mackie, who finally promises to escape to the country. But driven by his lust, he is unable to do without his customary visit to the brothel. Mrs. Celia Peachum bribes Jenny, and due to Jenny's and the whores' treachery, Mackie ends up in the hands of the police. For his convenience, he finds his old love Lucy Brown, the Tiger's daughter. It is thanks to her help that he manages to flee. Peachum bribes Brown, mentioning the possibility of his shabby beggars interrupting the upcoming royal parade, should Mackie not be arrested.

Mackie once again turned in; captured once again, this time with yet another woman. Precisely when his execution seems entirely unavoidable, however, the king's messenger delivers a plea for reprieve, including MacHeath's promotion to a status of financial security. The robber is reprieved through a strangely announced, artificially imposed and altogether unlikely happy ending, with the king's messenger in the function of a twisted *deus ex machina*. MacHeath's struggle for existence seemingly ends, but ends within a framework, which surely does not contend that all is well that ends well: *you see those in the light, but those in the dark are out of sight,* as the film *Threepenny Opera* concludes.

The Threepenny Opera illustrates the real by way of grotesque exaggeration, showing how the bourgeois is a criminal, and the criminal a bourgeois. Furthermore, it delivers a story in which the shady main character is not only spared, but promoted by the generous aid of even shadier figures. Corruption reigns supreme. And Brecht's play exhibits this fact in the twilight of bitter parody and culinary pleasure, and in a dramatic form that parodies the famous Romantic opera, which he judged as hackneyed. His first and foremost focus in *The Threepenny Opera* was on the criticism of social realities which cried for change.

The Threepenny Opera was written in collaboration with the composer Kurt Weill (with whom Brecht had already worked on *Mahagonny* in 1927), as well as with Brecht's reliable secretary Elisabeth Hauptmann, who translated Gay's English text into German. Although always in Brecht's shadow, Hauptmann was the one who had read about a re-staging of Gay's *The Beggar's Opera*, who had then obtained a copy of Gay's play, and who started translating it, handing scene by scene to Brecht. The characters of Gay's plays impressed Brecht to the degree that he thought they should be speaking his language and appear on the Berlin stage. Thus Brecht began rewriting Gay's text. Novelist and playwright Lion Feuchtwanger gave the play its title. The fact that Brecht inserted ballads by François Villon in Karl Klammer's translation without acknowledging the translator led to discussions of plagiarism instigated by Alfred Kerr. Tackling questions of authorship, originality, plagiarism, and collaboration, or limits of translation, appropriation and adaptation, however, would certainly lead too far. Suffice it to say that the lines are thin, and that "Brecht was a generous taker."

The generic classification of *The Threepenny Opera* is difficult. The labels opera or musical do not really work. The piece in nine scenes and a prelude is permeated by nineteen songs. Brecht referred to it as an attempt at epic theater. In the summer of 1928 *The Threepenny Opera* was composed as a play for singing actors, and as such was very representative for the artistic Berlin landscape of the twenties. It characteristically blends the most diverse elements of both verbal and musical composition. Brecht playfully combines

Lutheran German with slang and colloquial speech, easily adding
Anglicisms. And Weill skillfully blends Baroque tatters with elements
of popular music and with elements of the street ballad (*Moritat*) in
particular, as is the case with Mac the Knife's infamous ballad.

See the shark with teeth like razors.
All can read his open face.
And MacHeath has got a knife, but
Not in such an obvious place.

See the shark, how red his fins are
As he slashes at his prey.
Mac the Knife wears white kid gloves which
Give the minimum away.

But the Thames's turbid waters
Men abruptly tumble down.
Is it plague or is it cholera?
Or a sign MacHeath's in town?

On a beautiful blue Sunday
See a corpse stretched in the Strand.
See a man dodge round the corner . . .
Mackie's friends will understand.

And Schmul Meier, reported missing
Like so many wealthy men:
Mac the Knife acquired his cash box.
God alone knows how or when.

Jenny Towler turned up lately
With a knife stuck through her breast
While MacHeath walks the Embankment
Nonchalantly unimpressed.

Where is Alfred Gleet the cabman?
Who can get that story clear?
All the world may know the answer
Just MacHeath has no idea.

And the ghastly fire in Soho—
Seven children at a go—
In the crowd stands Mac the Knife, but he
Isn't asked and doesn't know.

And the child-bride in her nightie
Whose assailant's still at large
Violated in her slumbers—
Mackie, how much did you charge?

The Threepenny Opera's premiere took place at the *Theater am Schiffbauerdamm* in the Berlin of 1928, that is, very much unlike most premieres of Brecht's plays right where and when it was composed. It is the work through which Brecht became known. The piece was famous as a popular culinary experience, mainly due to Weill's catching music. Already after the premiere, something like a *Threepenny* fever took hold of Berlin. Even a *Threepenny* bar opened. Hotel jazz bands started playing Weill's music for the then common tea-time dance, and in the streets of Berlin, *Threepenny Opera* tunes were heard from the bow of every café fiddler. One could say with some sense of irony that the popularity of *The Threepenny Opera* was based on the audiences' misunderstanding Brecht's intentions. In *The Threepenny Novel,* his later version of the material, Brecht thematizes once again his real concern: the relationship of money to crime, of Capitalism to Fascism.

From its beginning in the late twenties, *The Threepenny Opera* occupied a firm place in the repertoire and one that it has managed to maintain to the present. At the end of the 1928–29 theater season, a total of four thousand and two hundred performances had been given. In 1931, a film version of the piece came out. By January 1933, the play was already available in various translations and had reached a total of over ten thousand performances all over Europe. But with Hitler's rise to power in 1933, the light of the vivid Berlin entertainment scene was radically extinguished. Thousands of Berlin artists left Germany to begin their lives in exile, including Bert Brecht and Kurt Weill, as well as Lotte Lenya and Marlene Dietrich. ❀

List of Characters in
The Threepenny Opera

MacHeath, nicknamed Mackie or Mac the Knife, the head of a criminal gang in London which specializes in robbery. He bases his work on deals with Tiger Brown, and is involved with Brown's daughter Lucy, while secretly marrying Peachum's daughter Polly. He is a shady character, known for his infamous ballad on successful criminality.

Jonathan Jeremiah Beggar Boss Peachum, the proprietor of the firm Beggar's Friend, an opportunist who abuses the poor for his own benefit, organizing London beggars district by district, and assigning them roles he wants them to play. He strictly disapproves of his daughter's marriage to Mackie and wants his arrest.

Celia Peachum, Peachum's wife, cooperates with her husband on Mackie's arrest by bribing Jenny and the other whores.

Polly Peachum, the Peachums' daughter, marries Mackie, means well with him and his affairs, warns him of the police, tells him to escape, and manages his gang in his absence.

Jack Tiger Brown, high sheriff of London and Mackie's friend since childhood.

Lucy Brown, Brown's daughter, a weak and gullible woman, and one of Mackie's loves.

Jenny cooperates with the other whores and delivers Mackie into the hands of the police.

Critical Views on
The Threepenny Opera

FREDERIC EWEN ON ESTRANGEMENT

[Frederic Ewen is the author of the Brecht biography entitled *Brecht, His Life, His Art and His Times*. He has also
written on Heinrich Heine and Friedrich Schiller. In this
essay he comments on the use of estrangement in the play.]

Did they draw a parallel between their own lives, outside the theatre,
and what they had just witnessed on the stage? Peachum's business
dealings that made use of piety and human pity as sources of
income; his and Mackie's collaboration with the police; the recip-
rocal betrayals—did not all these convey to the audience an indictment of its bourgeois morality? Did they not see in Mackie, the
"gentleman," a replica of the more respectable gentlemen with
whom they associated, and whose enterprises though grander, were
equally shady?

If they did not see all these things, the fault was not entirely theirs.
How could they be sure that the songs and sentiments expressed in
the play were not Brecht's, but those reflecting the bourgeois society
in which they were living? For actually, there are two Brechts within
the *Three Penny Opera*, and they overlap. There is the sky-storming
nihilist, laureate of the asphalt jungle; and there is the initiate into
Marxism, who was attempting to parallel the lesser duplicities and
betrayals, the thievery of the netherworld with the more seemingly
respectable but crasser and more thoroughgoing iniquities and corruption of the upper world. But could Mackie be taken seriously as
the exemplar of the contemporary "expropriating" bourgeois? And
what social content could be assigned to the injunction "not to be
too harsh on injustice, because it will perish of itself"? There was
nothing here to revolt any listener, except one already socially aware
that injustice *can* be done away with.

Brecht himself became conscious of the ambiguities in this work,
and in subsequent annotations tried to clear the air by insisting on
the close analogy between the character of Macheath and the
modern bourgeois. He instructed the actor to represent the highwayman as "a bourgeois phenomenon," with the bourgeois' regular,

almost pedantically meticulous social habits, such as visiting certain "Turnbridge coffee-houses." ⟨...⟩

Yet, despite inconsistencies and ambiguities, the *Three Penny Opera* represents a long step forward from *Baal* and *Drums in the Night*. Few works of this time so clearly mirror certain aspects of the twenties. Its acid irony, and parody of operatic sentimentality and make-believe are in keeping with the anti-sentimentalist demands of the period. Brecht had replaced the traditional and frequently meaningless operatic libretto with one that was easily accessible, highly poetic, yet realistic and contemporary in setting. He had also tried to achieve a "critical distancing" on the part of the audience, to replace the customary "primacy of feeling." He was employing a number of devices (later to be subsumed under "estrangement") such as establishing a deliberate dichotomy between words and music—brilliantly realized by Kurt Weill; separating the various elements of the play, such as action and song; utilizing projections of placards with biblical and other mottoes; direct addresses to the audience; and, not least, revolutionizing the character of the musical settings. The spectators were never left in doubt that they were in a theatre. Yet there was the traditional tie to and attraction of the old Singspiel of Mozart and the Viennese folk-comedy, of the cabaret, and the French vaudeville. ⟨...⟩

Brecht's *Dreigroschenoper* and Kurt Weill's musical score represented a critique not only of society but of drama itself, and the opera in particular. "Thus was created a new genre," Weill wrote.

—Frederic Ewen, "The Social Zoo: The Three Penny Opera," *Bertolt Brecht: His Life, His Art and His Times*. Ed. by Frederic Ewen (New York: The Citadel Press, 1967): pp. 175–77, 179.

WILLY HAAS ON THE PLAY'S TIMELINESS

[Willy Haas reviewed films and edited Rowohlt's magazine. In this excerpt, Haas comments on the play as a predictor of the time to come.]

It was the time of the early fad for "musicals" in Berlin. ⟨. . .⟩

In fact, the success of *The Threepenny Opera* was "in the air." Brecht and Weill had many models—but not only in 1728 London and 1928 Berlin. Brecht drew from the verses of the fifteenth-century vagabond-poet and highwayman François Villon. Again, as in *A Man's a Man*, Brecht wrote soldier songs in the style of Kipling's *Barrack-Room Ballads*.

All his models—Gay, Hogarth, Villon, and Kipling—can be sensed in the fabric of *The Threepenny Opera's* final version. As noted, Brecht was a *Literat* who rarely wrote without literary models.

And yet, his final creation was entirely original and contemporary, entirely in the style of the cynical 'twenties, entirely Berlin-West 1928, with its insolence, its Bohemian elegance, and its polished dialectic. At the same time, the play was a seismograph of the threatening future which—despite all cynicism, luxury, pleasure-seeking elegance, caustic wit, and the arrogance of a metropolis standing near the center of the cultural world—already foreboded the guillotine that was, a few months later after Black Friday at the New York stock exchange, to crash down on people everywhere. The songs of *The Threepenny Opera* get their reckless impact from cynicism at the brink of disaster—an impact still felt today. For it was this world crisis that brought Hitler on the scene, resulting in the Second World War and the collapse of old Germany. A foretaste of all this is evident in the songs of *The Threepenny Opera*, just as the cynical aphorisms of Chamfort anticipate the death of another epoch, the rococo, in the French Revolution. ⟨. . .⟩

The Threepenny Opera, of course, is a paean to cynicism, amorality, and anarchistic violence—it is indeed a paroxysm of delight over these. It remained for the platitudinous literary nit-pickers—to use a term of Rimbaud's much admired by Brecht and by us—to discover the supposedly soft, wounded heart of social compassion behind this thorny exterior.

—Willy Haas, "*The Threepenny Opera* and Its Consequences," *Bert Brecht*. Translated by Max Knight and Joseph Fabry (New York: Frederick Ungar Publishing Co., 1970): pp. 51–54.

KARL H. SCHOEPS ON ADAPTATION

[Karl H. Schoeps teaches in the German Department at the University of Illinois. Among his books are *Bertolt Brecht and Bernard Shaw* and *Bertolt Brecht*.]

The Threepenny Opera is perhaps Brecht's best-known and most widely played work. In John Gay's *The Beggar's Opera* Brecht found an ideal source and in Kurt Weill an engaging composer whose songs from *The Threepenny Opera* became extremely popular. One of them—"The Ballad of Mack the Knife"—became a top song on the American hit parade in the 1950s and is still well known today.

The setting for the opera is Victorian London. The opera opens with a prelude at a market in Soho. A ballad singer introduces the main character, Macheath, called Mack the Knife, in "The Ballad of Mack the Knife": "The shark he has his teeth/ In his face for all to see./ Macheath he has a knife/ But his knife cannot be seen." (Brecht called this ballad a "Moritat"—*Mord* means murder; *Tat* means deed. *Moritaten* were songs usually sung by street singers at fairs; the subject was usually a bloody and hideous crime.) ⟨. . .⟩

Gay's text used popular language and everyday scenes from life in London. The main character, Macheath, was modeled after two famous London criminals: John Sheppard and Jonathan Wild. Macheath's underworld enemy, Peachum, was given traits of Walpole himself. According to Gay, the message was: "High life equals low life." "Through the whole piece you may observe such a similitude of manners in high and low life, that it is difficult to determine whether (in the fashionable vices) the fine Gentleman imitates the Gentleman of the Road, or the Gentleman of the Road the fine Gentleman." ⟨. . .⟩

Brecht transferred the action from the 1720s to Victorian London and added a few ballads by the French highwayman-poet François Villon. Otherwise, he followed Gay's plot very closely. But his satiric attack was directed against a bourgeois society, not against the aristocracy which had been Gay's target.

The happy end serves not only as a parody of the *deus ex machina* of Greek tragedy (the gods who intervened to solve all problems), but also of the "unreal" and sentimental bourgeois plays that always ended happily. The character of Macheath is also a parody of the petit bourgeois: he has his regular habits (every Thursday night, without fail, he visits the brothel); he insists on all the trappings of a bourgeois wedding (he does not care how they are acquired); he has a bourgeois concept of art and bourgeois manners (he is appalled when Jacob eats fish with a knife); and, for him, marriage is mainly a means of protecting and increasing his business.

Brecht noted in 1935 that he wanted a distinct break between the musical numbers and the spoken parts. To achieve this, the orchestra is placed visibly on the stage. For each song, the actors change their positions on stage, the light turns to a golden color, a musical symbol is lowered from the loft, and the title of the song is projected onto a screen. To prevent the audience from becoming too involved in the progress of the action, and to direct its attention instead to the way in which the content is presented and the lessons contained, a summary of each scene is projected onto a screen before the scene begins.

In Gay's version, the capture of Macheath was a high dramatic point of the opera. Brecht, however, avoided this type of dramatic structure, which builds up to a climax, by having Macheath arrested twice.

—Karl H. Schoeps, "*The Threepenny Opera* (and *Happy End*) (1928)," *Bertolt Brecht* (New York: Frederick Ungar Publishing Company, 1977): pp. 115, 121–23.

STEPHEN MCNEFF ON THE QUESTION OF GENRE

[From his contribution to the *Cambridge Companion to Brecht*, Mcneff looks at the "operaness" of *The Threepenny Opera*.]

The Threepenny Opera is not, as I have said, an opera. Neither was its source. John Gay had set out to ridicule the taste for Italian Opera, which was at its height in London in 1728. There is some dispute about the significance of the anti-Walpole satire in *The Beggar's Opera*, but there is little doubt that it was a revolutionary work, 'a play about a social group that had never had a play written about them before'. For its first audience, it was a fresh and exhilarating experience, cleaning out the cobwebs in popular musical theatre of the time, and playing for sixty-two performances while making the fortunes of its creators and cast. The fact that later revivals (including the 1920 one) to some degree or other prettified the music to the point of emasculation does not seem to have deterred Brecht and more particularly Weill (there is no special evidence that Weill heard the 1920 score although no doubt he could have obtained a copy if he'd wanted to). Brecht clearly seized on the satirical and wider political possibilities of the original, and Weill was obviously in harmony with him in creating a work suited to the time. Weill would have been acutely aware of the satirical implications of a Beggar's or *Dreigroschenoper*. Even though his works were hardly conventional, his reputation had been largely established through the operatic medium and he would have understood the social and professional implications of a parody of the operatic system probably better than Brecht.

If later versions of *The Beggar's Opera* are regarded as essentially revamping John Gay's original, it would be wrong to think of Brecht and Weill's *Der Dreigroschenoper* simply as an adaptation. *The Threepenny Opera* is to all practical intents and purposes a new work. Perhaps one should properly say that it takes *The Beggar's Opera* as its model or inspiration. It would be dull to make a complete comparison here (even if space allowed), and a reading of both texts will soon make clear the differences in incident and location. What is more important to understand is that Brecht used *The Beggar's Opera* for his own purposes. As John Willett has mentioned, 'in Gay the target was an aristocracy whose affairs were much like those of the underworld; here (in *The Threepenny Opera*) it is a bourgeois society which allows there to be an underworld at all'. Actually, the precise authorship of *The Threepenny Opera* was a matter of some dispute at the time of its première. The original playbill merely acknowledges Brecht as 'adapter' with Hauptmann as translator and notes that there are interpolated ballads by François Villon and Kipling. Weill, however, does get sole credit for the music. This situation changed after the first publication of the libretto and Brecht became author of the work, but not before Brecht had to defend himself against charges of plagiarism for 'forgetting' to acknowledge one of the translators of the interpolated material—a fact which, as Stephen Hinton reminds us, led to Brecht's famous remark about 'fundamental laxity in matters of intellectual property'. Whatever the case, and there is no dispute that Brecht lifted various chunks from a variety of sources including his own work, the 'feel' of the eventual *Threepenny Opera* is of a fresh, original work even if, to use Hinton's useful term, it is a montage. ⟨. . .⟩

Brecht made no secret of his contempt for conventional opera and wrote vehemently about his attitudes to it. ⟨. . .⟩

At the risk of over-simplifying, Brecht's objections seem to revolve around the idea that opera, by the all-embracing nature of music and spectacle, tends to draw its audience into its emotion in an uncritical fashion—the experience of opera is purely one of pleasure without any higher judgement being required. This is as valid a criticism of conservative opera today as it was of opera in the Germany of the 1920s.

—Stephen McNeff, "The Threepenny Opera," *The Cambridge Companion to Brecht*. Ed. by Peter Thomson and Glendyr Sacks (Cambridge: Cambridge University Press, 1994): pp. 61–64.

Plot Summary of
Mother Courage and Her Children
(Mutter Courage und ihre Kinder)

Brecht's later work begins with *Mother Courage and Her Children: A Chronicle of the Thirty Years' War*. It was written in the fall of 1939 on the island Lidingo, during Brecht's Swedish exile. The piece is a rewrite of a motive taken from his earlier *Drums in the Night*. Brecht borrows the title character's name from Grimmelshausen, although Brecht's Mother Courage has rather little in common with the Baroque camp follower. But intensely inspired by Grimmelshausen's *Der Abenteurliche Simplicissimus Teutsch* (1669), Brecht was able to find in Grimmelshausen what he was deeply interested in: the historical color and detailed representation of the Thirty Years' War and its social consequences.

Mother Courage clearly qualifies as epic theater. The V-effects manifest themselves as narrative summaries given before the scenes are actually acted, or in form of the nine songs and numerous satirical splinters which successfully debunk the audience's expectations. Its frequent dialect adds to its difficulty as well as to its charm. The form of the play is anti-Aristotelian in the sense that it consists of a lose sequence of twelve illustrations, each of them introduced by a chapter heading. This makes for an open form, which as such lacks a clear beginning as well as a definite ending. The twelve scenes are set in Poland, Sweden, and Germany, and span the time frame from spring 1624 to January 1636. The play begins after the real beginning of the Thirty Years' War in 1618, and it ends before the war actually ended in 1648.

Many have posed the question whether *Mother Courage* is a tragic piece. Is Anna Fierling, nicknamed Mother Courage, a symbol of motherhood and a victim of the war, or rather a ruthless scavenger? Brecht would not give us permission to feel for her. But why then did he make her such an ambiguous figure? When the piece was first performed with Paul Burkhard's music in 1941 at the Schauspielhaus Zurich, Switzerland, the only European theater to stage Bert Brecht's work during the Second World War, the audience identified with the protagonist and began to feel pity toward her as an individual, which of course ran totally counter to Brecht's idea of estrangement. When in 1949 after his return from the United States Brecht himself directed a performance in Berlin, with Helene Weigel playing the lead, and with Paul Dessau's music, Brecht's epic intentions once again failed. Instead of exclusively thinking about how war is to be avoided, the spectators felt compassion for Courage, as if she were a character from real life. This escape into illusion was far less enlightened and enlightening than Brecht had hoped for, but it was at the same time far more than escape: it was the audience's fascination with "a symbol of supreme human tenacity."

The sutler woman Anna Fierling is a business woman who adapts to her times. She travels with her covered canteen wagon and tries to make the best of her situation, partly on the side of the Swedish Protestants, and partly siding with the Catholics. She is able to turn the war into her own business, but by that token unable to protect her children. While she manages to make a living from the war and its troops, she loses her two sons, brave Eilif and honest Swiss Cheese. Although Courage feels all these tragedies deeply, her main focus remains her business. Against the background of the cruelties of the Thirty Years' War, Mother Courage obstinately practices her materialism vis-à-vis the vicissitudes of this very war. Eventually, she is left entirely alone, pulling her wagon, worn out, isolated, poor, and yet stubbornly determined to continue on the given track—and to find her son Eilif, of whose death she remains innocent.

On the one hand, Anna Fierling is *clever*, as the play repeatedly points out. She is a rather fierce, highly opportunistic and not so easily affected woman, who sets out by traveling north, not only in order to actively seek the war, but also in order to commercially participate in it. She follows the war and makes it very much into her business. In this sense it is certainly not correct to exclusively depict her as an entirely innocent victim of the war. She is a brilliant businesswoman who chooses to take part in the Polish-Scandinavian war long before she actually moves on to the main area of conflict, the Thirty Years' War, in which Brecht's piece is chiefly set. In Courage's opinion, war is business, and good equals useful. For the sake of her business, she crosses over from the Protestants to the Catholics, fighting for her own faith in war. This is when her trade prospers and her theories on the war business are in full bloom. At the height of her career she sings:

Nobody try and tell me this is different
War's a business and it's just like all the rest
All right, we have to deal in guns and bullets
But it's still about survival of the best.

Nobody needs to go and be a martyr
If you're clever then there's no need to be brave
Keep moving, keep buying, keep selling, keep killing
The only peace you'll find is in the grave.

The war goes on. The war is raging.
The men are here. They must be fed
And what remains must now start trading
That's us. Let's go. It's going well.

On the other hand, Courage is the mother of two sons and a daughter, all three of different paternity. She is a mother, who in spite of her various intentions to stay outside of the war in order to protect herself and her children loses all three of them in the war and because of the war. When in the process of this war, all three children are killed, Courage returns to the Protestant side, and falls into a state of poverty in which survival becomes an urgent question. Brave Eilif is executed for his brutality, and all too honest Swiss Cheese dies for his loyalty. Courage's original pieces of war wisdom become increasingly absurd. Sparing one's children and at the same time surviving the war is staged as an enterprise that is doomed to failure. *Mother Courage* is not shown at a place and time when good or evil demeanor really seem to make any difference. War is not logic, neither is it justice. And Kattrin, the alternative character in the play who tries to rebel against the inhuman order of the war, and who manages to give warnings of a Catholic attack, is shot on the roof and pays with her life. Her heroism clearly demonstrates the horror of the situation, and Mother Courage's *Eia popeia* cradle song next to her daughter's body is in spite of Brecht's intentions a moving scene.

Brecht's *Mother Courage and Her Children* is theater of war in all senses. It is written and first staged during the Second World War, it is set in the Thirty Years' War, and it thematizes the devastating dynamics of the war business. Brecht discloses the lies about wars; his perspective is one from below. The heroes and heroines of war are not its leaders. This is the message. What Mother Courage does not learn is what the audience is supposed to learn. That in the 17th century as well as in the 20th, war is organized by the class in charge. That the dominated class is doomed to suffer through the consequences. That war is a uniquely horrendous form of business with different means. That it is destined to turn human virtue into something fatal. And that for war no sacrifice is outrageous enough. ❀

List of Characters in
Mother Courage and Her Children

Anna Fierling, about forty years old, nicknamed Mother Courage and the title character of the play, is a camp follower and a mother of three children by three different fathers. She loses all three children in the war, while surviving the war by selling supplies to both sides. She is a tenacious human being who neither wants nor gives compassion, a strong traveling businesswoman unable to save her own children. A poor loner by force, Courage is determined to continue her life. She is repeatedly characterized as clever.

Kattrin Haupt, Mother Courage's only daughter, became mute after one soldier's attack, and disfigured in the face after another. She has a kind heart and a strong capacity for compassion, which makes her an alternative character in this play. When she rebels against the inhumanity of the war by giving warnings of an attack, she is shot on the very roof from which she spoke.

Eilif Noyocki, Mother's Courage's elder, intelligent, and brave son, who joins the army and is first honored and then executed, and of whose death Courage remains innocent.

Swiss Cheese Feyos, Mother Courage's younger and honest son, who dies for his loyalty.

Yvette Pottier, an attractive young prostitute, whom Mother Courage uses as an example to try and teach her daughter Kattrin how to become tough. Yvette ends up marrying an old colonel.

Peter Lamb, a cook and Yvette's first seducer. Much like Mother Courage, he profits from the war before he inherits a Dutch tavern and offers Courage a share in it, which she refuses to accept.

The Military Chaplain, a dark demonstration of religion's role in war. He lives out of danger in the commander's service and uses his office to prepare soldiers for murder and death, repeatedly justifying the war as a religious enterprise which asks for sacrifice. ❀

Critical Views on
Mother Courage and Her Children

FRANZ N. MENNEMEIER ON THE PHILOSOPHY OF SONG

[Franz N. Mennemeier has written on Friedrich Schlegel, on modern German drama, and on the drama of exile.]

Two songs, above all, illuminate the "philosophical" basic gestus of the play: Mother Courage's "Song of the Great Capitulation" in the fourth scene and the "Song of the Wise and Good." The first song, functioning as advice to the young, brawling soldier and connected in this way to external dramatic action, is a lyrical résumé of the scene: it points to the inner structure of the whole drama at the same time. In the temporal stream of epic theater there is a momentary intimation of a life beyond oppression as a utopia. The prerequisite for an alteration of existing conditions would be the "great" anger. Clearly people do not feel such anger. Behind the promisingly wild, revolutionary saber rattling of the soldier cheated of his tip a very "small" anger becomes quickly visible. The whistle of a subordinate officer is sufficient to restore in the mechanism order and obedience that have been briefly disturbed and to nip in the bud the rebellious impulse of the soldier inexperienced in reunuciation. But Mother Courage is experienced. Her "Song of the Great Capitulation," full of maternal sympathy for the "little" capitulation of the soldier, describes the course of life as inevitable disillusionment of all individual impulse to "higher things," as the inevitable erosion of all personal desires for happiness. The picture of the music band recurring in the refrain, in which one winds up marching, "keeping in step, now fast, now slow / And piping out our little spiel," underlines the gray opportunism, the wretched "accommodation to people" to which the human being is reduced by the process of existence. The pious proverb ("Man proposes, God disposes"), turned by Brecht into its opposite by a slight twist, a mere change of punctuation and stress ("Man proposes: God disposes"), recurs also from stanza to stanza, summoning up the picture of a world in which small, human plans collapse because the whole lacks planning and guidance. The poem drags along with it, like a heap of old rubbish, the devalued slogans of petty-bourgeois, pious activity ("All or nothing," "I am the master of my fate," "You can't hold a good man down," "Where there's a will there's a way").

The theme of the Great Capitulation is also treated in the "Song of the Wise and Good," which the cook and Mother Courage sing when the sutler woman's business has been totally ruined by plague and famine, and nothing remains but beggary. In altered form the song appeared already in *The Threepenny Opera:* there it occupies a somewhat inorganic position within the dramatic context. The charm of the passage in the drama at hand lies in the natural interaction of the lyric and dramatic planes. From stanza to stanza, the text of the song is more advanced than interrupted by the home-baked reflections of the cook—a chanting, logically inarticulate sing-song in prose. These reflections have a semipublic character; they are asides, as it were, and sanctioned by a "public" verse form, combine impressively into an emotional whole with the message of the song. For Brecht, the virtuoso of language, it is a masterly achievement of alienation. The popular ballad form expands into an unspeakably melancholy, subtly humorous litany of the despoiled creature and of the senselessness of human effort. It is a song sung as though from a distance and still of a direct, elementary expressive power. The song was awkward for Marxist critics because of its apathetic character. Here a deep, pessimistic side of Brecht, associated with death and transitoriness, becomes visible; a "Biblical" sadness wells up, which again and again thwarted his stubbornly maintained faith in progress; it is this sadness to which Brecht owes his best inspirations.

Despite the melancholy, a subtle humor carries through the song that is itself highly novel within the framework of the popular ballad. Bert Brecht permeates and alienates the elementary lyricism of the lament with a surface structure of logic. The cook must apply his song about the person of great virtue to his own particular case. In this process comical "leaps" occur, which reflect the absurdity of all attempts to bring sense into the senseless and chaotic course of the world. ⟨. . .⟩ This lamenting, lyrical, reflective style, which makes the inexactitude of popular reasoning fruitful for artistic purposes, usually serves Brecht as a means of social criticism. But in the song under discussion it seems to be concerned to make language itself relative. It is "alienated" to the chatter that is not only the jargon of a cook but represents the speech of even the most intelligent man when he becomes conscious of the extent of the catastrophe of life. The concepts of virtue in the song, moreover, are not exempted from the process of alienation. The poem uses them as formulas emptied of meaning, as moral *topoi* connected with semilegendary, semihistorical personages (the "wise" Solomon, the "daring" Caesar, etc.). Like the song of the Great Capitulation, the "Song of the Wise and Good" also emphasizes the speed of decay: ⟨. . .⟩ The moralizing scheme suited to the popular ballad style reveals a deeper metaphysical meaning. Behind the rational, pragmatic appeal to morality and the argument of morality, the natural sound of existence is hidden: lament for the transitoriness of what exists and the insignificance of human works, the good as well as the bad.

—Franz N. Mennemeier, "Mother Courage and Her Children," *Brecht: A Collection of Critical Essays.* Ed. by Peter Demetz (Englewood Cliffs, N. J.: Prentice-Hall Inc., 1962): pp. 141–43.

ROLAND BARTHES ON GESTURE AND DISTANCE

[Roland Barthes (1915–1980) was a French social and literary critic, whose writings on semiotics made structuralism one of the leading intellectual movements of the 20th century. He authored 17 books, countless articles, and is considered one of the great contemporary thinkers.]

In particular, the Pic photographs throw light on the Brechtian notion of distancing [*Verfremdungseffcht*] which has bothered the critics so much. Brechtian distancing has called forth passionate reactions: one critic condemns it while at the same time denying that it exists; another pretends to find it again and again in quite different dramatists, while at the same time holding Brecht responsible for it. These contradictions are perfectly normal, for to criticize distancing is always proof of the existence of a prejudiced anti-intellectualism: one fears that the spectacle will be impoverished, will freeze to death, if the actor does not shed on it the fire of his body, the lavishness and the warmth of his "temperament". But anyone who has seen the Berliner Ensemble or who looks at the Pic photographs even for a moment knows perfectly well that to distance in no way means to act less. Quite the contrary. The verisimilitude of the acting has its origin in the objective meaning of the play, and not, as in "naturalist" dramaturgy in the truth inherent in the actor. That is why, in the long run, distancing is not a problem for the actor, but for the director. "Dispassionately, without involvement!" Brecht says to his actors, doubtless wishing to purge them of their petty personal emotions before letting them act. Put differently, to distance is to cut the circuit between the actor and his own pathos, but it is also, and essentially, to re-establish a new circuit between the role and the argument: it is, for the actor, to give meaning to the play, and no longer to himself in the play.

I should like to give some examples of this new relationship, based on some of the photographs of *Mother Courage*, from Act 1. The objective meaning of the play is what Brecht calls the social gesture and that is the political test; I want to show how the detail of the gesture has a political meaning, rendering properly and correctly the differing alienation of the roles. Men are not each exploited in the same way: that is one of the essential meanings of Brechtian theatre, and it is this sort of differential ideology that distancing throws light on and makes evident. This is what distancing is: to fulfill the true purpose of a play where the meaning is no longer the actor's truth, but the political relationship of situations. In other words, distancing is not a form (which is precisely what all those who want to discredit it say it is): it is the relationship of a form and a content. In order to distance, there has to be a reference point: the meaning. ⟨. . .⟩

The theatre to which we are accustomed is a theatre of the second degree. It is a gesture which imitates another gesture—Clytemnestra or Niobe, to turn once more to the example of the Mater Dolorosa, are illustrations of a grief which had already been made theatrical before the theatre took possession of them; and it is because passion is itself a form of theatricality that our classical stage, over several centuries, has been so fond of it. Brecht, however, does not imitate passion, which is already theatricality in life, but action itself. This approaches the classical epigones of Aristotle, since for Aristotle, as for Brecht, the character has to follow from the action and not the action from the character. Thus, all that we see of Mother Courage is not offered (faked, one might say) as expressive, but only as functional. Yet, as the expressiveness of roles has become for us one of the greatest delights of theatre, we tend unceasingly to reconvert the deed into meaning, the act into gesture, doing into being, the epic poem into tragedy. What a fine spectacle, that of a mother who defends her offspring like a lioness defending her young! (One sees in the comparison an indication of this second theatre of which I have just spoken.) What is new in Brecht is that his theatre, far from complacently making use of the theatre of life, destroys this theatre in the theatre itself, substituting for it the Essential Mother, a functional mother. Ceasing to imitate the imitations, Brecht returns to the transitive contents of human action.

—Roland Barthes, "Seven Photo Models of Mother Courage," *The Drama Review* 12 (1967): pp. 44–45, 52.

CHARLES R. LYONS ON THE BUSINESS OF WAR

[Charles R. Lyons was professor of English and Drama at Stanford University. He had an extraordinary faith in teaching the right combination of dramatic theory and performative practice. His books include *Bertolt Brecht: The Despair and the Polemic, Critical Essays on Henrik Ibsen, Samuel Beckett,* and *Shakespeare and the Ambiguity of Love's Triumph.*]

From the poet's point of view, Anna Fierling, the scheming sutler woman, is unambiguously guilty. In the opening scene, Brecht uses the "Song of Mother Courage" to project an attitude—Anna Fierling's response to war as an arena for commerce. On the narrative level, the song is the hawking cry of the sutler woman; as a *gestus* however, it projects her own use of war and a coldly realistic attitude towards life itself, an honest confrontation with the inevitability of death. The presentation of this image is amplified by the sergeant and the recruiting officer, whose description of conflict extols war as a time of organization and efficiency in which a man can find his identity in fulfilling a useful function. ⟨. . .⟩

⟨. . .⟩ It is demonstrated with some clarity that both Mother Courage and the soldiers are motivated by necessity, committed to the logic of exploitation in order to survive. In their discussion, the nature of Fierling's identity as Mother Courage is defined. ⟨. . .⟩

Again and again in this play, there is an insistence upon the fact that absolute values do not obtain in human experience—even more pessimistically, that one cannot put trust in any human agreement because men are greedy and fickle. Mother Courage herself becomes the clearest image of that greed. Brecht's ethical position is clear in this initial scene: Mother Courage loses her sons to the Recruiting Officer because her impulse to conduct business—to sell the belt to the sergeant—distracts her attention. The final summary speech of this scene contains the central irony of the play:

> *When a war gives you all you earn*
> *One day it may claim something in return!*

The system which sustains Fierling and her family is, in reality, a destructive force to which she also will be subject. ⟨. . .⟩

In the first scene, Mother Courage loses her son to the army because she is seduced by the recruiters into conducting business instead of guarding against the threat of induction. In the third scene of this play, in a bold confrontation of reality, Mother Courage haggles over the bribe needed to free the captured Swiss Cheese, and the delay caused by her haggling results in the swift execution of her son. However, Fierling's haggling in the painful experience of Scene Three is an image of far greater complexity than the more simple bargaining of the first scene. It is not a pure greed which motivates the delay that causes the death of Swiss Cheese; the sutler's wagon, which is at stake, is the means of existence for Mother Courage and Kattrin. When she is aware that the cash box is gone, Courage tries to hold on to a sum great enough to "pack a hamper and begin over," declaring "It won't be the end of the world." When she is finally aware of the desperateness of the situation, she is, of course, willing to lose the entire two-hundred guilders, but it is too late. ⟨. . .⟩ Compassion, in Fierling's imagination, is a matter of purchase. But all human action is not directed by financial transaction. Unwilling to cast all away for the life of her son, Mother Courage loses him. However, her error is not primarily an error in motive but rather an error in judgment—the application of her business *courage* to a situation in which such haggling was inappropriate, indeed, fatal. ⟨. . .⟩

With the single exception of Kattrin's compassionate and suicidal act, the primary sense of humanity in *Mother Courage and Her Children* exists in the bond which unites the little family, embodied in Fierling's desperate and futile efforts to hold them together. However, these efforts are made according to a realistic logic in which vows and promises are empty; in which the only bond that unites men is the exchange of items in a commercial transaction. In her commercial dealings, Courage sees people not as human beings, but in one of two categories: victims and persecutors. And she exercises compassion only in her treatment of Eilif, Swiss Cheese, and Kattrin. There is an irony in the fact that the little human community of Fierling's family is, to a strong degree, seen by Mother Courage as objects which belong to her. They seem to exist for her as commodities. Certainly she has strong feeling for them; yet they seem to her to be things which she owns more than individual and unique beings. ⟨. . .⟩

War, in Bertolt Brecht's epic imitation of the religious wars of the seventeenth century, becomes a metaphor for business. In Brecht's terms, the war itself is the business of the big men who manipulate politics for their own advantage, exploiting mankind, and this ethic of exploitation pervades the social structure, making man's relationship with man primarily a business relationship. Brecht's image of the war as big business is clarified in a conversation between Mother Courage, the chaplain, and the cook. ⟨. . .⟩

⟨. . .⟩ Courage cannot cut herself free from her parasitical dependence upon the war. She is distraught when "peace has broken out" and she is left with a wagonload of goods in a deflating market: "Dear old peace has broken my neck." ⟨. . .⟩ ⟨W⟩ith the return of wartime business, she celebrates the war as a protective institution, one which supplies and cares for its people, providing as it does ample opportunity for exploitation and plunder: ⟨. . .⟩.

To read *Mother Courage* primarily as an antiwar poem is a mistake, limiting its significance and its relationship to the Brechtian canon. The state of war in this play is the state of the human condition: it is the greed and exploitation of the cities of Chicago and New York as they exist in *In the Jungle of the Cities;* it is the organized destruction of identity in *A Man's a Man;* the exploitation of the suffering proletariat in *The Measures Taken.* In this world, the assertion of the will in an honest action is suicidal. ⟨. . .⟩

The image of Anna Fierling, the Mother Courage who has lost all three children to the destructiveness of war, strapped to her wagon in order to go forward once more into her life of trade, prompted the sympathy of Brecht's audiences and irritated the playwright who saw so clearly that Fierling was the focus of an unambiguous guilt.

—Charles R. Lyons, "Mother Courage: Instinctive Compassion and The Great Capitulation," *Bertolt Brecht: The Despair and the Polemic* (Carbondale and Edwardsville: Southern Illinois University Press, 1968): pp. 90–92, 95–97, 99, 101–2.

ROBERT LEACH ON ABSENCE OF SYNTHESIS

[Robert Leach is a freelance writer and freelance theater director. He also teaches acting. Among his books are *A History of Russian Theatre* and *Boy and Baggage*.]

Brecht's 'dialectics' in *Mother Courage* are quite different from Lukács's. Instead of the synthesising of form and content into the whole and rounded work, Brecht presents a spikier, looser number of components which interact dialectically but never synthesise. Brecht believed that Marx's analysis denied the sort of graspable, perhaps static, reality implicit in Lukács's conception. For Lukács, reality was governed by underlying forces which were beyond human control, indeed almost beyond human understanding, but for Brecht this was mystification which vanished when a work's *function*, which Lukács's analysis never contemplated, was considered. Brecht wanted his theatre to intervene in the process of shaping society, so that Lukács's duality of form and content was replaced (to over-schematise briefly) by a triad of *content* (better described in Brecht's case by the formalist term 'material'), *form* (again the formalist term 'technique' is more useful here) and *function*. In Brecht's dramatic form, these three constantly clash but never properly coalesce to compose a rounded whole. (This can be illustrated by the way Brecht's plays tend not to have conventionally acceptable endings: Mother Courage's problems are by no means resolved at the end of this play.)

Thus Brecht's concept of the work's function radically affects his dramaturgy. He is not content to accept, as Tolstoy was, for example, the author's unquestionable omniscience with regard to the reality presented. (Tolstoy's attitude to the Napoleonic Wars may be compared instructively with Brecht's attitude to the Thirty Years War.) Brecht is interested in the author's own relationship to that reality. He sees certain events, and certain attitudes displayed, and uses them as the starting-point. Incomplete, perhaps, they provide gestures ('material') with which to begin. As Walter Benjamin explains,

> The gesture has two advantages over the highly deceptive statements and assertions normally made by people and their many-layered and opaque actions. First, the gesture is falsifiable only up to a point; in fact, the more inconspicuous and habitual it is, the more difficult it is to falsify. Second, unlike people's actions and endeavours, it has a definable beginning and a definable end. Indeed, this strict, frame like, enclosed nature of each moment of an attitude which, after all, is as a whole in a state of living flux, is one of the basic dialectical characteristics of the gesture. This leads to an important conclusion: the more frequently we interrupt someone engaged in an action, the more gestures we obtain. Hence, the interrupting of action is one of the principal concerns of epic theatre.

The 'interrupting of action' we may describe as the 'technique'. It is specifically the interrupting which Eisenstein called 'montage' and Brecht called 'epic theatre': 'it is the retarding quality of these interruptions and the episodic quality of this framing of action which allows gestural theatre to become epic theatre', Benjamin concludes.

The technique of interrupting is active and interventionist. For the actor, it is the justification for the Brechtian rehearsal exercise 'Not this . . . but this . . . ', and for the audience, it is the means by which the world is seen as changeable, the rise of Arturo Ui as resistible. Imperceptibly, these remarks about technique have led to a consideration of the function of Brecht's theatre, which is to 'learn how to see and not to gape, To act instead of talking all day long'. The interruption therefore is thoroughly 'indiscreet' (a favourite term of Brecht's: the music in *The Threepenny Opera,* he said, was to be a sort of 'copper's nark'), serving as a means not only of pointing up something which a socialist realist play would flow over, but pointing it up in such a way as to energise the spectator, to stimulate her or him into an awareness of the possibility for change. Thus, if fragmentary events or attitudes culled from real life form the starting-point for Brecht's play, becoming involved in it, taking part in it, is its end.

Mother Courage is an almost programmatic illustration of this alternative kind of dialectical theatre, because its power derives precisely from the relationship between the material, the technique and the function, the 'gesture', the 'interruption' and the 'stimulation'.

—Robert Leach, "Mother Courage and Her Children," *The Cambridge Companion to Brecht.* Ed. by Peter Thomson and Glendyr Sacks (Cambridge: Cambridge University Press, 1994): pp. 130–31.

ROBERT POTTER ON REWRITING *MOTHER COURAGE*

[Robert Potter is a professor in the department of dramatic arts, the University of California Santa Barbara. In this excerpt, Potter writes about the play and what it was like to transplant it.]

The Los Angeles of the 1940s we lived in wasn't exactly a cultural desert, but it came pretty close. To be there as a refugee, as so many were, was to be down on your luck—despite the sunshine and the palm trees. What an unlikely place for a radical German playwright and director to spend the war, trying to crank up his broken-down career. ⟨...⟩

Brecht, who was nobody's fool, dealt calmly with his own subpoena. Charming, wheedling and lying his way into the good graces of the Un-American Activities Committee, he accepted their bemused thanks for his cooperation, and flew off the next day to Germany where (armed with the scripts of his undiscovered masterpieces) all his dreams were to come true. ⟨...⟩

Mother Courage, after all, was an icon—a classic that was European down to its gritty fingernails. The role had been defined—for all time, it seemed—by the gaunt peasant features of Brecht's actress wife Helena Weigel. The play seemed to me untouchable

⟨...⟩ Brecht's great play, categorically anti-heroic, has an affectionate understanding for the circumstances of ordinary soldiers, and a deep contempt for the grandeur of the generals and emperors who send them off to get themselves (and sometimes the generals and emperors too) killed in dubious battles. ⟨...⟩

To call Mother Courage a tragic figure—as I unflinchingly would insist that she is—is not to say that she is a saint or a martyr. Quite the reverse; her suffering is pointless and preventable, like the warfare off which she lives. ⟨...⟩

Transplanting the play to America was great fun, and in truth not that difficult to do. ⟨...⟩

A brief look at Scene Six of Brecht's play may give some idea of the effects of these territorial shifts. ⟨...⟩

For all of its tragic overtones, *Mother Courage* is also a lyric work by a great poet, incorporating lyrics to a dozen songs. Here I decided to preserve, as much as possible, the formal meter and rhyme schemes of Brecht's original lyrics, and search for American melodies of the Civil War era to which they might be fitted. Fortunately there are thousands of published songs from that period to choose from, everything from familiar Stephen Foster airs to popular songs, sentimental ballads and spirituals. This aspect of my version provides a very different set of textures than the dark settings of Paul Dessau's music for the Berliner Ensemble production. Instead of compounding the darkness of the original lyrics, I sought to counterpoint them with light hearted, optimistic-sounding American music—an irony I think (or at least hope) that Brecht would have appreciated. ⟨...⟩

As for Brecht, he seemed to nod knowingly and give me a wink of encouragement every now and then, for old times' sake, as I labored to reimagine his story in its new American setting, back there in the hot summer of 1979. And why not? His own work was characterized by adaptation (or some would say, appropriation) from start to finish. Brecht knew that old stories, parables and historical events had in them the stuff of stirring contemporary dramas, provided that they were reimagined and refocused to throw light on contemporary circumstances as well as perennial dilemmas.

—Robert Potter, "Writing Mother Courage," *The Brecht Yearbook* 24 (The International Brecht Society: University of Wisconsin Press, 1999): pp. 15–20.

Plot Summary of
The Good Woman of Sezuan
(Der Gute Mensch von Sezuan)

The Caucasian Chalk Circle and *The Good Woman of Sezuan* are Brecht's most important parable plays. He wrote *The Good Woman of Sezuan* between 1938 and 1940, that is to say in various stages of his exile, and in collaboration with Ruth Berlau and Margarete Steffin. The first production took place in 1943 in the *Schauspielhaus* Zurich. The play is set in pre-war China, in Sezuan, the capital of the Szechwan province. It is built of ten scenes, interludes, and an epilogue. The homeless water-seller Wang and the poor prostitute and later shopkeeper Shen Te are the only good people in the parable, and the only ones who communicate with the useless gods. Much more markedly than with the more ambiguous Mother Courage, Brecht demonstrates with the character of Shen Te that charity and mildness lead to ruin under the given social and political circumstances.

In order to justify their divine existence, the three gods descend from heaven to earth, in order to search for a good human being. The gods become weary of their not all too promising quest, and upon entering the city of Sezuan, they ask the water-seller Wang for someone who could give them a shelter for the night. Nobody in the whole town seems willing to put them up, with the exception of the prostitute Shen Te, who kindly offers them a place to rest. She even sends a client away, so as to be able to provide them with a room. For the strong parabolic illustrations of good and evil in the play, it is crucial that in contrast to her reputation, Shen Te has a kind heart. The gods are very pleased with her hospitality, so that the following morning they reward her with a gift of money, with which the good soul is finally able to switch to a more respectable profession: She now rents a tobacco shop.

As soon as the news about her shop is spread in Sezuan, a entire legion of supposed extended family and debtors contact her. In her tobacconist's shop, she becomes increasingly more convinced that being good cannot be reconciled with her survival. For her protection, the gentle-minded Shen Te assumes the identity of a ruthless male cousin by name of Shui Ta, who is harsh and fierce enough to drive the parasites away. Then Shen Te meets Yang Sun, an unemployed airman. She saves him from suicide and falls in love with him. Shen Te and Yang Sun plan a marriage. But when Yang Sun is alone with Shui Ta, Shen Te's alter ego, he candidly speaks, as it were, from man to man, admitting that he is only greedy for Shen Te's money and has no sincere interest in her. This is how Shen Te loses her fiancé.

When she is about to close down the shop, she learns of her pregnancy. Only under the mask of ruthlessness can the good woman of Sezuan provide for herself and her unborn child, so that Shen Te is said to be out of town, and Shui Ta is asked to reappear in the shop. The merciless and selfish cousin restores Shen Te's fortunes in no time. He starts a tobacco factory, crowns himself *tobacco king*, and hires the ex-airman Yang Sun, who faces no troubles in becoming a foreman, since he is an equally merciless exploiter of the factory workers. Wang, who has been appointed messenger by the gods, and who keeps them posted on Shen Te's situation, becomes terribly worried due to her extensive absence. He suspects Shui Ta of having killed her. Shui Ta is arrested, and the gods themselves appear as judges.

Thanks to Shen Te, who thinks that the gods mean well, and who feels her growing inability to wear the mask of evil and bear her double existence, the gods eventually manage to disentangle the situation in a court scene, where Shen Te reveals herself by tearing off her mask and disclosing her disguise. The foolish gods are in a state of rapture about the fact that the good soul still exists, and nonchalantly return to heaven without settling the poor woman's problem. When the painfully split character tries to draw their attention to her serious dilemma, they entirely avoid the issue, telling her that one way or the other she will live her life. All they are willing to offer is their ridiculous floating off on a pink cloud, leaving Shen Te in her state of absolute despair carelessly behind them. After their success in finding what they needed, in order to restore their image in an evil world, they part, singing a valedictory hymn to praise Shen Te, but to praise her for their own sake:

> *What rapture, oh, it is to know*
> *A good thing when you see it*
> *And having seen a good thing, oh,*
> *What rapture 'tis to flee it*

Be good, sweet maid of Setzuan
Let Shui Ta be clever
Departing, we forget the man
Remember your endeavor

Because through all the length of days
Her goodness faileth never
Sing hallelujah! Make Shen Te's
Good name live on forever!

Even though Brecht's subsequent epilogue insists that the world as one in which the good die young cries for change, the question what needs to be done about Shen Te's quasi-schizophrenic dilemma remains wide open. Is it in vain that she cries for help immediately before and immediately after the gods' selfish song? Is it in vain that she loves her neighbor, her man, and her child? And what about exploitation of labor? Thinking about possible answers to these questions is a task the audience receives in the epilogue. It is likely that Sezuan stands for all places, and it is certain that Brecht encourages the audience to find an ending that makes a difference. ❀

List of Characters in
The Good Woman of Sezuan

Three Gods, useless, foolish, nameless deities who do not see human misery, and who descend from heaven in order to find a good person. Their search remains unsuccessful until they ask for a shelter and Wang commends Shen Te.

Wang, a homeless water-seller who naively trusts the gods' power. He is appointed messenger by the gods, and faithfully keeps the gods posted on Shen Te's situation.

Shen Te, the good woman, a poor prostitute and later shop-keeper. With the exception of Wang the only good-hearted character in the play. Her charity leads to her ruin under the social and political circumstances in question. She provides a shelter for the gods, and is the best of hearts. She saves Yang Sun from suicide and falls in love with him. Since goodness and survival are not compatible in the setting she lives in, she temporarily assumes the identity of Shui Ta.

Shui Ta, Shen Te's male mask or alter ego, her so-called cousin, who has a strong sense for ruthless business and exploitation of labor, and who ends up as the proprietor of a tobacco company, crowning himself tobacco king.

Yang Sun, an unemployed airman who is saved from suicide by Shen Te. As a foreman in Shui Ta's factory, he is greedy, merciless, and selfish, as is the proprietor.

Mrs. Yang, Yang Sun's mother who speaks in stereotypes and is as ruthless as her son

Shu Fu, barber and wealthy capitalist

Mrs. Mi Tzu, house owner and tobacco merchant

Mrs. Shin, widow

Lin To, carpenter

Ni Tzu, child ❀

Critical Views on
The Good Woman of Sezuan

[Eric Bentley, a major force in American theater, is known for his criticism as well as for his own plays, but above all for his work on Brecht and his translations of Brecht's work into English. Among his books are *Alfred's Lover, Playwright as Thinker,* and *Bentley on Brecht.* He first met up with Brecht at UCLA in 1942. Bentley performed *Threepenny* music in clubs.]

Perhaps all good foreign plays should be published first in a very literal translation and subsequently in various attempts at a true equivalent, even, if necessary, in "adaptations." Some plays can have high literary quality in another language and at the same time be fairly literal transcriptions. ⟨. . .⟩ Brecht toyed with the idea of his plays always being literally translated for publication and freely adapted for performance. But even this is not a perfect formula. Whenever the stage version is more plausible, has more character, more charm, vivacity, edge, or whatnot, reasonable readers will prefer it not only in the theatre but in the study: for it is more readable. Hence, when I had to discard the literal translation of *The Good Woman* for stage purposes, the nonliteral text that resulted was adjudged preferable by publishers and readers as well as producers and spectators. For the Phoenix Theatre production (New York, 1956) I decided to ignore the literal translation altogether and, working again with the German, to make a completely new rendering for the stage. Since all the larger libraries have copies of the first Minnesota edition, anyone who is curious about this can look up for himself what the differences are. The 1956 text does amount to "adaptation" in the sense that some passages have not been translated at all but deliberately omitted or changed. Luckily, the author was still alive when these changes were proposed, and when I last saw Brecht (June 1956) he approved them in principle. (He was not interested in inspecting the script line by line and probably was not well enough to do so in any case.)

In English, things have to be said more tersely than in German. Hence, English translations from German should always come out shorter than the original. Sometimes that is a matter of phraseology only: each sentence should come out shorter. But at other times the very thought and substance of a German text has to be made more compact in English, and in this case whole sentences of the original have to go. Now once you start this more drastic kind of "cutting" you also find yourself obliged to bridge the "gaps" you have made with new writing. This is one of the ways in which translation becomes adaptation. . . . It did so in the reworking of *The Good Woman*, and those who wish to know exactly what Brecht said in every detail will, as I say, have to go to the German or the first Minnesota edition. ⟨. . .⟩

For stage purposes, I found that everything in *The Good Woman* had to be said more briefly and swiftly in English than in the German, and I think the reader too will appreciate a terser, lighter textured piece of reading matter. I would not make this identical statement about *The Caucasian Chalk Circle*. It is not an easier play to turn into English, but it is far less abstract and more poetic. Consequently, the obligation to keep each phrase is far greater, and the result of keeping each—or nearly each—phrase seems a gain, rather than a loss. This does not mean that as soon as one has written out an "accurate" translation one has finished work. There remains an endless labor, this time not of trimming, cutting, and reshaping scenes, but of weighing one word against another, one phrase against another, and, finally, of trying to achieve a style that might serve as *the* style of this play. The renewed work on *The Good Woman*, since the method meant going back to zero, seemed more radical and while it lasted was indeed more intensive, yet in the end even more work may have been put in on *Chalk Circle*, though this work was done a little at a time and was wholly a matter of details. (A work of art is an accumulation of details.) ⟨. . .⟩

One has always to ask of a Brecht translation what German text it is based on, since Brecht himself was forever changing what he wrote. The present English versions are in principle based on manuscripts supplied by Brecht in 1945. This fact explains one or two things that might otherwise appear anomalous. For example, "Sezuan" was a city in the manuscript, though later it would be identified as "Szechwan," which is a province. Since Brecht obviously could not have had in mind a province when he wrote "a city," I consider the original reading sounder and have kept it. It is in line with all Brecht's other "misunderstandings" of geography and even with a stage tradition that goes back to things like the "seacoast of Bohemia" in Shakespeare.

—Eric Bentley, "Introduction," *Parables for the Theatre.* Ed. by Eric Bentley (Minneapolis: The University of Minnesota Press, 1948): pp. 9–11.

JOHN FUEGI ON THE QUSTION OF GOOD AND EVIL

[John Fuegi is professor of Comparative Literature at the University of Maryland. His work concentrates mainly on the 20th century, but he has also written on Medieval mysticism. Among his books are *The Life and Lies of Bertolt Brecht,* and *Brecht and Company.* He has received various film awards.]

The profound metaphysical question of why evil is permitted, indeed encouraged, in the world has seldom been asked with such force. With his usual genius for finding the appropriate specifically dramatic gestus to point his question, Brecht creates the split character of Shen Te/Shui Ta. Totally incredible in terms of fourth-wall style theater, her change from the "good" and very naive Shen Te to the "bad" and exceedingly clever Shui Ta, unrecognized by anyone but the petty blackmailer Mrs. Shin, is credible only within the dungheap Utopia, the nowhere and everywhere of Sezuan. The ancient convention of the impenetrable disguise is exploited in Brecht's non-realistic parable to its fullest dramatic and tragic potential. The quintessence of both the best and the worst facets of Mother Courage (businesswoman and mother), Shen Te/Shui Ta draws us close to her in pity and makes us recoil in fear. The closing scene of the play, where Shen Te cries out to the gods for some relief from the nightmare of this mad and vicious world, has much of the power of the scene in *Mother Courage* where the dumb drummer Kattrin pays for goodness with her life. It is no wonder that Reinhold Grimm asks of *The Good Person of Sezuan:* "Does not at least this play advance into the realm of tragedy?" One wonders if Brecht, had he himself produced it, would have sought to prevent identification with Shen Te. The play as the Ensemble and other theater groups have produced it has been magnificently unsuccessful in eliciting a cool response from audiences east or west of the Berlin wall. It is no wonder that this play has become (in terms of number of productions and performances) the most popular play in the whole Brecht canon. ⟨. . .⟩

As is usual with Brecht's plays of the exile period, *The Good Person of Sezuan* is so carefully constructed that it is difficult to imagine it beginning or ending later or sooner than it in fact does. The opening scene serves as a model of compact exposition. Wang has waited, so we learn, three days for the three gods to appear. We the spectators, however, are only forced to wait as long as it takes for Wang to complete some essential exposition. We should not be asking ourselves while we wait why Wang has not utilized the three days to find suitable lodgings for the expected gods. Then, with a promptness reminiscent of the arrival of Agamemnon, or of the witnesses at the trial of Oedipus, or of the wagon of Mother Courage, the gods arrive. By the end of the first scene, Brecht has sounded every essential theme of the play at least once. The goal of the gods has been clearly explicated as has the reason for their embarking on a search for a "good person." The necessary "good person" is found in the opening scene. We are given a foretaste of the problems that goodness brings with it, as she must give up a customer in order to help the gods. Through Wang's first fruitless attempts to find lodgings, we have been given a panoramic view of the general heartlessness that prevails in the city of Sezuan. And, just before the gods exit in the first scene, Shen Te clearly states the problem which the rest of the play will illustrate. She cries (and in this beginning is her end): "Of course I would like to be happy, to follow the commandments, to honor my father and my mother, and to be truthful. Not to lust after my neighbor's house would be a joy for me, and to be faithful to one man would be a pleasure. Also, I do not want to exploit any one or to rob the helpless. But how am I to do all this? Even when I fail to keep a few of the commandments, I can hardly survive." After the fairy tale-like and wholly inadequate gift of the one thousand silver dollars (given at the insistence of the ever practical and cynical third god), the gods exit. They exit hastily, in precisely the way they will exit at the play's close, waving goodbye, and mouthing their impossible sentiments drawn from an outmoded humanist tradition. Just as we have seen with *Mother Courage* and we shall see with *Galileo,* all following scenes in *Sezuan* have been precisely anticipated in the opening scene. Like these other two plays, *Sezuan* proves to be classically circular in structure. And again as with these other two plays, this perfectly rounded aesthetic construct with its highly schematized world view will provide no philosophically or economically viable answers. Again we must content or discontent ourselves with a dramatic statement of an important and fundamentally human problem.

This talk of fundamental human and moral problems conjures up an image of a play perhaps forbiddingly Teutonic. And yet this it is not. The way in which Brecht has seasoned what might well have become a most unappetizing dish is a classic study of fulfillment of Horace's dictum, that the artist should combine the useful and the pleasurable. A key ingredient that Brecht uses to offset the taste of the wormwood he serves us (and something that Brecht criticism thus far has made surprisingly little of) is humor. Whenever the text begins to bog down, Brecht manages to lift it up again with the judicious use of his sense of the sheer absurdity of much of what we say and do. For the person attuned to Brecht's humor (and perhaps it is an aquired taste), Wang's opening monologue on the gods is typical. We find that Wang has learned of their coming, not from the traditional oracle, but from a buyer of cattle! When Wang finally spots the gods, he does not recognize them by their traditional "godlike" qualities but by the simple fact that they show "no sign of having any occupation at all."

—John Fuegi, "Brecht and the Oriental Stage I: *The Good Person of Sezuan*," *The Essential Brecht* (Los Angeles: Hennessey & Ingalls Inc., 1972): pp. 133–136.

SIEGLINDE LUG ON THE PLAY'S FEMINEST POTENTIAL

[Sieglinde Lug is professor of German and Comparative Literature at the University of Denver. Her books include *Poetic Techniques and Conceptual Elements in Ibn Zaydun's*

Love Poetry. She has written articles on Brecht and others, with a focus on the post-war era and women writers.]

The Western tradition of putting woman on a pedestal in an imagined, not real framework, represents a male dream of something perfect outside himself. The most influential poet of German literature continuing this myth of woman as the guiding principle and representative of absolute goodness and purity is Goethe, with his much quoted Eternal Feminine. When Faust enters Gretchen's bedroom, he finds merely an orderly girl's room, but the restless man projects a dream of everything that is not in himself onto its atmosphere. To mention some key concepts from his monologue, this dream mixes girlish sacred purity, tranquillity, bliss, order, contentedness, motherliness—the image of a heavenly angel. Since all these qualities are not in him, they are projections of his psychological needs, an idealistic image of what he—sometimes—yearns for, a beautiful myth. Simone de Beauvoir defines the relation of this myth to reality: "Thus, as against the dispersed, contingent, and multiple existences of actual women, mythical thought opposes the Eternal Feminine, unique and changeless. If the definition provided for this concept is contradicted by the behavior of flesh-and-blood women, it is the latter who are wrong: we are told not that Femininity is a false entity, but that the women concerned are not feminine."

Critics have often referred to *Faust* as an influence on Brecht, but the parallel to Goethe's *Iphigenie* seems more obvious when one considers *Der gute Mensch von Sezuan.* Both works, with women as protagonists, focus on the idea of how to be absolutely and consistently good in the face of pragmatic considerations. ⟨. . .⟩

In Brecht's drama *Der gute Mensch von Sezuan,* the sex-neutral word *Mensch* refers to a woman, thus suggesting the cliché that goodness per se is represented by a woman; at least such is the surface appearance. Although the prevalent view is that Shen Te cannot survive in pure goodness, I am inclined to examine more closely how good her goodness actually is in this drama and for whom. Her goodness does not appear as a positive capacity, but as a negative inability, that is, she cannot say "no." Sun, her lover, puts that in the cynical context of her behavior as a prostitute. Shen Te herself defines it as the "Verführung, zu schenken." Thus her will to do good does not arise from a moral conviction which then could be trusted but is merely the easiest way for her, the path of least resistance and of finding most approval. ⟨. . .⟩

By splitting the one person into stereotypical "masculine" and "feminine" aspects and showing that polarity as destructive and deceitful, Brecht—consciously or not—makes suspect the cliché of the constructive and healing quality of polar contrasts in men and women. In answer to Brecht's question in the Epilogue whether we need a new person, a new world, or different gods, the prevalent reaction by critics has been to point to social circumstances alone and call for a different world. That answer is based on the assumption that Brecht's Marxist convictions require economic solutions or changes of systems. Looking at the intrinsic message of the drama, however, the Shen Te/Shui Ta division appears as a major issue in itself, which is linked to the economic one, not subordinated to it. It seems that a more viable person would be one who can balance and integrate the qualities of Shen Te and Shui Ta.

—Sieglinde Lug, "The Good Woman Demystified," *Communications from the International Brecht Society* 14, no. 1 (November 1984): pp. 4–5, 7.

Roland Speirs on the Play's Parabolic Strength

[Ronald Speirs teaches in the German Department at the University of Birmingham. His work is mainly in the field of Euopean Modernism. He has written on Brecht, Kafka, Thomas Mann and has a forthcoming edition of Friedrich Nietzsche's *Birth of Tragedy*.]

⟨. . .⟩ Having made 'a great step backwards in technique' with *Galileo, The Good Person of Szechwan*, written 'for the bottom drawer', was to be based much more uncompromisingly on the principles of Epic Theatre.

The genre of parable lent itself to Brecht's conception of 'demonstrational theatre' in a number of ways. The parable, so he explained to Walter Benjamin, was a form of writing in which the imagination was kept accountable to reason, the tendency towards autonomy of the aesthetic impulse being held in check by the obligation to write what was useful. For Brecht it was a genre that aimed at transparency: the surface of specific events and characters served to point beyond (or behind) itself towards general, 'abstract' meanings it illustrated 'concretely'. Because it does not pretend to be anything other than a made-up story, clearly told to advance an argument, parable has the kind of naive relation to reality that Brecht thought was an important quality of Epic Theatre; the opposite of naiveté in this sense is naturalism, where the artist seeks to create the illusion that what his work shows is reality.

Although Brecht began writing parables before he became a Marxist, it was a genre that gained in importance for him once he had adopted this ideology. This was because Marxism is concerned not only to establish 'the laws of social life' (*die Gesetze des menschlichen Zusammenlebens*), but also to assert the divergence of what is 'true' from what is 'real'. For the Marxist, the truth about humanity is not simply a matter of what is observably the case. This is because he believes that human potentiality has never been able to find its fullest expression within historical actuality, because of the fact that men live in an alienated condition within societies founded on class-division, competition and exploitation. *The Good Person of Szechwan* is an example of a parable which illuminates a 'truth' that could never be established by describing life naturalistically, because the 'good person' in each of us supposedly disappears at an early age under the pressure of the alienating conditions of everyday social existence. Thus, Brecht's *Fabel* invites the audience to consider an exception in order to make it understand the rule.

In *The Good Person*, what Brecht called the 'element of parable', the artifice that makes it clear that the play is not pretending simply to mimic life, is constituted by the arrival in the Chinese province of Szechwan of three Gods in search of a good person whose existence will justify the continued existence of the world as it is. The play thus presents itself from the outset as a re-working of an ancient, but very familiar motif, thereby advertising its own literariness and promoting a reflective response from the audience by inviting it to compare the familiar story with the new and, as it turns out, strongly parodistic, version. The search of the Gods serves to lead the audience through a process of learning or enquiry into the question that has driven them from the peaceful 'higher' regions down to earth, the question, namely whether it is possible for a human being both to be good and to survive. In the end, the enquiry becomes a judicial one, the court scene being one of Brecht's favourite devices for recapitulating and explicitly debating the issues raised by the events of a play. ⟨. . .⟩

Brecht once made some interesting remarks to the critic Ernst Schumacher concerning the parable. Praising the fact that it presented the abstract concretely, Brecht called it 'the most cunning' of forms. As an example he cited the case of Lenin, who once gained support for the Bolshevists' controversial New Economic Policy with the help of a short parable entitled 'On the Climbing of High Mountains', the moral of which seemed so self-evident to his audience 'that they simply swallowed the theoretical part of his argument whole' ('*daß sie das Theoretische mitgefressen haben*'). The 'cunning' of Lenin's parable lay in its substitution, by way of analogy, of a relatively simple problem for a much more complex and less clear-cut one, and also in its emotive, suggestive association of politics with the heroic activity of mountain climbing. Lenin's parable, in other words, was a classic instance of the rhetorical deployment of the imaginative qualities of the genre for purposes of persuasion. *The Good Person of Szechwan* is a more extended example of the same rhetorical procedures.

—Ronald Speirs, "The Good Person of Szechwan," *Bertolt Brecht* (London: MacMillan, 1987): pp. 138–40, 145.

ELIZABETH WRIGHT ON MASQUERADE AND OPPRESSION

[Among Elizabeth Wright's books are *Postmodern Brecht: A Re-Presentation* and *Lacan and Post-Feminism*.]

Shen Te is split into the good exploited female and bad exploiting male. In her first masquerade, as Shen Te, she is attractive for her very helplessness and innocence, while as Shui Ta, her second masquerade, she is attractive for her power. Divided by her masquerades, she occupies the hysterical position in that she performs (both in the sense of functioning in and acting out) the historically specified form of symbolic identification. On the whole Brecht's female characters are shown as admirable to the extent to which they develop their 'womanliness' into a form of political strength—there is a long list of motherly figures, apart from 'the Mother', which includes Kattrin, Grusha, Frau Sarti (in *Galileo*). But Shen Te starts her masquerade with a handicap: as a prostitute she masquerades as a fantasy object. Although for Brecht her profession 'demonstrates' economic necessity ('Let me admit: I sell myself in order to live'), for the gods, to whom she makes this admission and who cautiously pay her for their overnight lodging, she is a lure and forbidden source of (obscene) enjoyment: 'But please let nobody know that we paid. It might be misinterpreted'.

These considerations are necessary in dealing with Brecht's presentation of a person, who would be (essentially) good, were it not for the prevailing economic conditions: 'I should certainly like to be, but how am I to pay my rent?' Her doubts rest on the fact that she is a prostitute, albeit with the traditional topos of having a heart of gold. For Brecht her ego is thus not alienated by its very constitution, since a self is presumed outside or before an alienation has taken place. This alienation is produced because 'something is wrong with this world of yours': 'To be good while yet surviving / Split me like lightning into two people'. The question posed by the play is, however, not what is good or what is bad, but whether it is possible to *be* good in the world as it is at present. ⟨. . .⟩

Brecht is clear in his exposure of the bourgeois capitalist order and its gods who go along with it. As a prostitute Shen Te is on the lowest rung of the ladder in that she herself is the commodity. With the financial backing from the gods she attains petit-bourgeois status as a shop-owner, a rung above the workers, while the previous shop-owners, alienated from their own class, sink to the *Lumpenproletariat*, the refuse of all classes. Through Shen Te, Brecht demonstrates that a successful business in the capitalist world depends on taking rather than giving. To balance the giving of the 'good' person, a 'bad' person is needed to take it back, just as in *Puntila* the 'drunk' generous side of the landowner is a trade-off for the 'sober' mean side.

What is missing from this analysis is an examination of the material conditions of gender behaviour outside its relation to class. The prostitute Shen Te is forced to sell her body for money:

an early version of the play was called *Die Ware Liebe*, 'commodity love', to resonate with the notion of 'Die wahre Liebe', 'true love'. To get the newly impoverished Shen Te out of this double-bind, the police officer advises Shui Ta to find a rich suitor, the barber Shu Fu—in other words, to sanctify the sale of herself by entering into a marriage contract with a single willing buyer: 'you can't earn your living by love, or it becomes immoral earnings . . . respectability means, not with the man who can pay, but with the man one loves . . . all you need do is to find a husband for her'. So far, so good. Brecht has made the same point in *The Threepenny Opera*: bourgeois marriage is a form of legalised prostitution. What is omitted from this critique is the relation of class oppression to sexual repression. Albeit by dint of omission, the play also 'demonstrates' that the advantages accruing to men from the subordination of women are not merely confined to class: neither 'cousin' Shui Ta (were he a 'full' presence), nor lover Yang Sun, nor protector Shu Fu, not to speak of the gods, are likely to offer any support for Shen Te's child. ⟨. . .⟩

It is hardly surprising, then, that feminists feel that Marxism regards itself as a form of Master-knowledge, one that 'takes the position of the subject, the knower, and its radical "partner", such as feminism, is assigned the role of object of knowledge'. Being locked in 'dichotomous thinking', Marxism tends to prioritise the first term on the basis of the logical paradigm A/not-A, where A affirms and not-A negates. With the Shen Te/Shui Ta dichotomy Brecht has merely reversed this in making Shen Te represent the affirmative—'she can't refuse', or 'say no' (the negative pole of power), whereas Shui Ta specialises in the negative (the positive pole). This opposition is soon sublated into a new greater dichotomy of active male professional conquerer-son and passive female proletarian mother, 'demonstrating' the assumption that while the division of classes is a fact of history, the division of sexes is a fact of nature: women just *are* mothers, while men are (high) flyers.

Shen Te is placed in a subordinate position by a number of different systems and not just by a single mechanism—that of a woman with property within capitalism and its market economy. Her oppression is economic as a prostitute, psychic as a romantic beloved, social as a pregnant mother. There is here an ensemble of social practices that mutually reinforce one another.

—Elizabeth Wright, "*The Good Person of Szechwan:* Discourse of a Masquerade," *The Cambridge Companion to Brecht.* Ed. by Peter Thomson and Glendyr Sacks (Cambridge: Cambridge University Press, 1994): pp. 118–19, 121–23.

Plot Summary of
Galileo
(Galileo Galilei)

Brecht's *Galileo* has three versions, and it tends to appear under various titles: *Galileo, Galileo Galilei,* and *(The) Life of Galileo.* In its final version, which was written after the dropping of the atomic bomb in Hiroshima, the play is composed of fifteen scenes and, untypical for Brecht's plays, of only one song. *Galileo* is often considered as Brecht's most intellectual play. Brecht and Margarete Steffin wrote the first version in Denmark in 1938–1939. The play had its premiere at the *Schauspielhaus* Zurich in 1943. It was collaboratively translated into English by Charles Laughton and Bert Brecht in California.

Set in Italy in 1609–1637, it is a piece about the Italian astronomer and physicist Galileo Galilei (1564–1642), who is famous for his insistence on insight, new knowledge and an often unpleasant truth. *Galileo* is not only an anti-Aristotelian play in its Brechtian epic form, but also in its content. Galileo copied the Dutch invention of the telescope and used it to establish Copernicus's theories in opposition to the Aristotelian world picture, proving that the sun and not the earth is the center of the universe.

The play opens in the year 1609, when Brecht's Galileo lives with his daughter Virginia, his housekeeper Signora Sarti, and her little son Andrea, who already as a child shows clear signs of developing into a promising student. Galileo is a lecturer at the University of Padua near Venice, but since the Venetians underpay him and do not leave him sufficient time and room for his research, he accepts an offer from the Grand Duke of Florence. During his committed research Galileo finds evidence for the solar system, but although the papal astronomer Clavius confirms Galileo's findings for the fact that the earth is not the center of the universe, the Florentine monks as well as the philosophers at the Medici court refuse to accept the claim's truth value. The holy office radically denounces the idea of a solar system as heretical questioning of the cosmic order, especially because a disposition such as Galileo's is very likely to soon query the religious and social order as well. As a consequence, Galileo Galilei falls into eight years of silent isolation.

And yet he cannot resist the current researches into the nature of the sunspots. When Cardinal Barberini, an enlightened mathematician, becomes the new Pope, Galileo sees a slim chance for his new science. But he neither supports nor protects Galileo, whose highly subversive ideas begin to circulate. As a consequence, the Medici deliver him to the Inquisition in 1633. The Grand Inquisitor persuades Pope Urban VIII that such discoveries undermine the authority of the Church. Galileo is shown the instruments of torture, and scared into abjuring his theories in public. On June 22, 1633, Galileo's students, among them Andrea Sarti, refuse to believe that Galileo would ever recant his teachings. The bells, however, announce that he has recanted. Galileo enters as a broken man. His students are nonetheless shocked at his cowardice. In scene 13, Andrea famously says: *unhappy the land that has no heroes*, and Galileo equally famously replies: *unhappy the land that needs a hero*.

From then on, Galileo lives in the country, silent, isolated and controlled by the Inquisition. He spends the remainder of his life with his daughter, whose fiancé broke off the engagement because of her father's scientific fervor. And he writes his *Discorsi* under the strict eye of the church, which confiscates the manuscripts as soon as they are written. But Galileo secretly keeps a copy. Although disgusted at Galileo's former act of cowardice vis-à-vis the church, Andrea Sarti decides to pay the old man a visit before leaving for Holland. When Galileo hands him the completed manuscript of his *Discorsi*, Andrea's contempt instantly becomes admiration. Now he understands why Galileo has recanted, namely in order to be given the time to complete the work he believed in. In the end, Andrea Sarti is the one who smuggles Galileo's *Discorsi* over the border.

Brecht admires Galileo as one who dares to be critical of the status quo. The only striking song of the play is sung in scene 10. Although it seemingly ridicules Galileo, it has an ironic basis which turns the tables and opposes mistress and maid in a new and revolutionary Brechtian order:

When the Almighty made the universe
He made the earth and then he made the sun.
Then round the earth he bade the sun to turn—
That's in the Bible, Genesis, Chapter One.
And from that time all beings here below
Were in obedient circles meant to go.

Up stood the learned Galileo
And told the sun: Stand still!
From this time on, the wheels
Shall turn the other way.
Henceforth the mistress, ho!
Shall turn around the maid.

Galileo is a unique play in Brecht's oeuvre in that it takes a well known historical person as its protagonist. Is Brecht's play history or simply a twisted historical reference? Brecht only pays respects to the historical accuracy in the rough outline of the play. The rest is fiction. He invents some of Galileo's opponents, and shapes them to his liking. He updates Galileo's reasoning so that it can be a contribution to the secularization of thinking as exemplified by Marx. Brecht became interested in the historical Galileo in his early exile, when he was thinking about friends and colleagues who had remained in Germany. And something like an underground political worker, searching for the truth against the erring Hitler regime might well have been on his mind.

But Brecht also equips Galileo with traits of a hedonist who needs to see himself as a criminal, whose cowardice has set a pattern for the future practice of science, since he has submitted science to authority, rather than asserting its right to change the world to the better. And in Hiroshima science was irresponsibly used for the worst.

Why did Brecht choose historical material at all? To then show how he feels limited by it? Not even Brecht can possibly have believed that a scientist of the 17th century, whose friends were priests, was actually a proto-Marxist and took his views as socially revolutionary. Although it is tempting to do the opposite, it is essential to keep in mind that *Galileo* is a play, not history. By its mere definition it is fiction, not fact. Brecht was not a historian, but referred to himself as *Stückeschreiber*, as a writer of pieces, as a playwright. His masterpiece *Galileo* demonstrates Galileo as a passionate scientist, who not only enjoys eating, but for whom the quest for knowledge and insight is pleasurable for the senses. This alone presents Brecht's theory of the didactic and at the same time culinary theater in a nutshell. ❀

List of Characters in
Galileo

Brecht's title character **Galileo Galilei** is a forty-five-year-old astronomer and physicist, who lives with his daughter Virginia, his housekeeper Signora Sarti and her bright son Andrea Sarti, lectures at the University of Padua near Venice, and is a subject of the Venetian Republic. Galileo is a fat hedonist and enthusiastic scientist, gluttonous for wine as much as for truth. Underpaid at Padua, he accepts an invitation to the Medici Court in Florence, where during his research he finds evidence for the solar system, a discovery which the church calls heretical, so that Galileo falls into a state of silence and isolation, but takes up his research again and presents his results. He is scared into abjuring his theories, and from then on lives in the country, secretly keeping a copy of his famous *Discorsi,* whose main manuscript the Inquisition confiscates as Galileo writes it.

Andrea Sarti, Signora Sarti's eleven-year-old son and Galileo's eager student, whom the master treats like a son, and who already as a child shows clear signs of becoming a promising scholar. Andrea considers his master a coward when Galileo recants his teachings. Only later when he visits Galileo on his way out of the country, he understands why Galileo acted the way he acted. Andrea is the one who initiates the masterwork's international fame by smuggling a copy of the manuscript of the *Discorsi* across the Italian border. He ends the piece by introducing young men to scientific reasoning, just as Galileo began it by introducing Andrea to his science.

Virginia, Galileo's pious daughter who does not care about her father's work, nor would she understand it if she cared. As a consequence, the father's demeanor around his daughter demonstrates little care and interest. Virginia is engaged to Ludovico Marsili for a period of eight years. At the play's conclusion, however, Virginia is forty years old, lives with her father, and bears the consequences of his decisions.

Signora Sarti, Galileo's housekeeper and Andrea's mother, is highly practical, and absolutely devoted to Galileo's and Andrea's welfare.

Ludovico Marsili, a rich son of reactionary aristocrats, for a time Galileo's student, and Virginia's fiancé, before he breaks off the engagement due to Galileo's teachings and behavior vis-à-vis the Inquisition.

Cardinal Barberini, a liberal mathematician who is on friendly terms with Galileo. But when Barberini becomes Pope Urban VIII, he too lives under the pressures of the Inquisition and plays along with the interrogation of Galileo as ordered by the Inquisition. ❀

Critical Views on
Galileo

[Philosopher Günter Rohrmoser has written on Shake-speare, Lessing, Nietzsche, and Brecht. Among his books is *Nietzsche Und Das Ende Der Emanzipation.*]

There are three versions of *Galileo*. Brecht wrote the first in 1938–39 in Denmark; it was published by Suhrkamp as a theater script and performed in Zurich in 1943. The second, American version was written in 1945–46 during the translation of the play into English which Brecht undertook with Charles Laughton, who played Galileo in 1947 at Beverly Hills, California, and in 1948 at New York. Finally the third version, which is based upon the English one, was written during Brecht's rehearsals on the stage of the *Schiffbauerdamm Theater* in Berlin. The essential difference between the individual versions is the ending, which is concerned with judging the figure of Galileo, his submission to the Inquisi-tion, and answer to the question about the beginning of modern times and a new age.

The 1938 version shows Galileo as an old man who outsmarts the Inquisition and, simulating blindness, completes his work and has the results smuggled out of the country by one of his pupils. Thus the cunning of reason triumphs also in the ethic of the scientist's political action, it is as far ahead of its century as his knowledge is, and causes a light to dawn in the darkness of his age. "I insist that this is a new age. If it looks like a blood-stained old hag, then that's what a new age looks like. The burst of light takes place in the deepest darkness." In the version of 1947 the last sentence, among others, has been deleted, just as in general the judgment upon Galileo has become harsher. Now he practices science like a vice, secretly and without any obligation to humanity. Galileo retracts his doctrines out of cowardice, and his contributions to the progress of science do not outweigh his failure to human society. Because of Galileo's failure in succumbing to sensual temptation, the new age, which emerges as a real possibility on the horizon of history, is no different from the dark ages of the past. Modern science, in itself an instrument of progress, transforms itself into a force for oppression in the hands of the rulers to whom Galileo has delivered himself.

There is no possible doubt that Brecht altered his view of Galileo and the historical importance of his scientific discoveries under the influence of the atomic bomb, which was developed and first dropped on Hiroshima during the creation of *Galileo*. Brecht could not ignore the fact that the atomic bomb with its fateful possibilities was a product of the science founded by Galileo at the beginning of the scientific age. In 1938–39 German physicists succeeded in splitting the uranium atom; in 1945 the atomic age began to exhibit its destructive possibilities; and in 1945 Galileo answers the question, "Do you no longer believe that a new age has begun?" this way: "Quite. Be careful when you pass through Germany with the truth in your pocket." ⟨. . .⟩

⟨. . .⟩ It is true even in the earliest version that the perspective in which Bertolt Brecht views an event of the past is oriented to the present and its oppressive problems. ⟨. . .⟩ What fascinates Brecht primarily in the historical problem of the beginning of a new age is the abstract aspect of a situation still concealing within itself all possibilities, and the courageous feeling of a man who has complete trust in the situation because he has not yet tested its strength against reality. ⟨. . .⟩

Galileo's life embraces a twofold responsibility: first to the work to be achieved, and then to the society to which this work is committed and which it seeks to serve. Can the two requirements be reconciled or do they stand in an irreconcilable contradiction to each other? If it is characteristic of a new age that society as a whole begins to move and the unquestioned oneness of the individual with its institutions begins to dissolve, then such a society offers Brecht an excellent model on which to demonstrate his basic propositions. ⟨. . .⟩ ⟨H⟩ow does this obviously changing interpretation in the several versions relate to the artistic and dramatic structure of the work? If it were possible to interpret the play as a revue-like, "epic" chronicle striving for colorful details, our final judgment on Galileo's life would indeed be a matter of indifference. For then the structure of the play would pursue the theatrical goal of reproducing his biography as such. The same would be true if the play were concerned with the interpretive dramatization of a complex character. Both possibilities are rejected. In turning to history Brecht is concerned in substance with the basic historical and human problem of his own age, which he is certainly correct in calling a scientific one. Galileo does not interest him as a character, but as a case.

—Günter Rohrmoser, "Brecht's *Galileo*," *Brecht: A Collection of Critical Essays*. Ed. by Peter Demetz (Englewood Cliffs, N.J.: Prentice-Hall Inc., 1962): pp. 117–20.

M. A. COHEN ON HISTORY AND MORAL

[In this excerpt Cohen discusses whether or not historical works can be separated from the moral they try to convey.]

For those who seek clear-cut literary definitions, historical drama is an elusive category. The many plays to which this description might be applied vary greatly in their degrees of historical involvement. ⟨. . .⟩

However, in *The Life of Galileo*, historical pretensions are clearly central. The play is perhaps best regarded as a "history" in something like the Elizabethan sense. ⟨. . .⟩

Galileo is so firmly grounded on historical re-creation that it is not always easy to separate the special pleading from the authenticity. We may agree that "it does not so very much matter whether the play is historically accurate, the moral is what counts," and yet find it difficult to isolate the moral from the history. Indeed it is arguable that the most important message of the play is essentially historical, that moral and history coincide, though what Brecht is most essentially "saying" in the play has been interpreted in a variety of ways. Whatever view we come to take, it seems likely that an analysis of the crucial manipulations of accepted fact in *Galileo*, of the points where Brecht most clearly exceeds his historical brief, is a useful accompaniment to an exploration of the moral.

That Brecht strove hard to obtain authenticity in many areas of the play is well known. The background reading and consultations which he undertook have been described, especially his attempt to think his way back into the Ptolemaic world picture. Much of the biographical matter is reasonably authentic too, despite the obvious omissions and distortions made in the interests of Brecht's characterization of the great scientist. ⟨. . .⟩

Comprehensive fidelity to fact would of course be an unreasonable demand to make of a play. ⟨. . .⟩

⟨T⟩here are ⟨. . .⟩ aspects of the real man ⟨Galileo⟩ which Brecht did not attempt to depict, even in an approximate sense. ⟨. . .⟩

An essential strand in the play's meaning is Galileo's relationship with the people; he believes in them as the future standard-bearers of science—astronomy will be talked about in the marketplaces and will be welcomed there. Against Sagredo, who accuses him of confusing the people's "miserable cunning" with reason, Galileo invokes the everyday common sense of "the mariner who, when laying in stores, thinks of storms and calms ahead" or "the child who pulls on his cap when it is proved to him that it may rain. . . ." These are his hope because they all listen to reason (Scene 3). In Scene 9 Galileo explains why he wants to write his works in the vernacular for the people who work with their hands: ⟨. . .⟩.

The point at which Galileo most clearly identifies the cause of science with that of social revolution is in Scene 14. The full implications of Galileo's long speech here are seldom recognized in comments on the play. Spalter, for example, dismisses the speech as "extrinsic" to the work as a whole, on the grounds that it contradicts the characterization of Galileo which has been developed previously. Spalter sees Galileo as a person whose "distinction is precisely that nothing can make him subordinate his lust for pleasure to categorical imperatives," his scientific activities being simply another expression of the "same basic drive for pleasure that makes Galileo a connoisseur of food and wine." Hence Galileo's final affirmation of the need to put the social responsibilities of the scientist before self-interest is unconvincing, because "one cannot build up a persuasive pattern of episodic detail and then expect to add a climax unprepared for by such detail without confusing the issue."

It is difficult to reconcile the final version of *Galileo* with Spalter's description. The bulk of his most interesting study is devoted to a tradition in German drama which he relates to Brecht's work, that of Lenz, Grabbe, Büchner, Wedekind, and Kraus. Brecht's early plays seem to fit in well, but it would seem that, in order to assimilate the later ones too, Spalter has, among other things, over-simplified

Brecht's characterization of Galileo and perhaps under-estimated the revision of the original conception by the third version of the work. In the play as Brecht left it, in *Stücke,* VIII, there is no question of the speech in Scene 14 being "extrinsic" nor of Galileo's nature being adequately defined in terms of "lust for pleasure." Galileo's sensuality, hedonism, and occasional dubious ethics (as in the matter of the telescope) are merely some facets of a many-sided character. We also meet the idealist whose faith in human reason strikes the sceptical Sagredo as naive: ⟨. . .⟩. Above all, there is the Galileo who affirms: "I say to you: he who does not know the truth is merely an idiot. But he who knows it and calls it a lie, is a criminal." ⟨. . .⟩

⟨. . .⟩ So far from being an extrinsic attitude in the play, this is the culmination of a theme which runs through the whole work, from the first major speech with its reference to the common people's discovery that the rulers have legs like their legs, to the rejoinder made to the Little Monk in Scene 8, and later the important speech made by the Inquisitor: ⟨. . .⟩.

⟨T⟩he moral ⟨. . .⟩ takes precedence over the historical representation. But what conclusions are we invited to draw ⟨. . .⟩. ⟨T⟩he self-indictment in Scene 14 must be taken with reservations, for the discriminating spectator ought to bear in mind the consequences of scepticism among the ignorant and feel that the Galileo who recanted was more realistic than the Galileo who wishes he had stood firm. ⟨. . .⟩

⟨. . .⟩ "The bourgeois class . . . knows very well that its rule would come to an end if the scientific eye were turned on its own undertakings. And so that new science which was founded about a hundred years ago and deals with the character of human society was born in the struggle between rulers and ruled." It would seem, then, that what Galileo has betrayed in the play is partly science in the sense of the science of society, which, in Brecht's view, meant Marxism. Pure science triumphs as Andrea smuggles the *Discorsi* over the border, but the penetration of social relations by scientific thinking, a potential age of reason, has been postponed. We do not have to endorse Brecht's equation between Marxism and social science to appreciate that his point about Galileo is a subtle one. When he speaks of the atomic bomb as the end product of Galileo's contribution to science and failure to society, he is holding Galileo responsible for two reasons: first, he contributed to the science that made the bomb; and second, he failed to help the cause of scientific thinking about social relations, which could have created an idealized age of reason in which the bomb would never have been made. ⟨. . .⟩

Galileo, like its Elizabethan predecessors, is a didactic history play which demands detailed exploration of its message. Unlike the Elizabethan histories, it also has pretensions to a degree of historical authenticity in the modern sense. No amount of factual support for its historical interpretation will make it a better play nor necessarily make the moral more acceptable, but, since the historical claims are made, and since so much of the moral content is historical moral, it is desirable that the history should not be a travesty.

—M. A. Cohen, "History and Moral in Brecht's *The Life of Galileo,*" *Contemporary Literature* 11, no. 1 (Winter 1970): pp. 80–83, 86, 90–91, 93–7.

BETTY N. WEBER ON REVOLUTION IN PERMANENCE

[Betty N. Weber taught Germanic studies at the University of Texas.]

In *Galileo* the playwright rearranges church history, the initial thrust of Protestantism, and the devastating consequences of counterreformation in the seventeenth century to parallel the history of the old Social Democratic Worker's party in Russia through waves of revolution and reaction in the twentieth century. In making such an analogy Brecht follows the well-established practice of measuring contemporary events against historical models. Since Marx and Engels, every episode of social upheaval has been meticulously compared with events of the French Revolution. One of the most celebrated books to employ this type of analogy appeared only a few months before Brecht began writing *Galileo:* Leon Trotsky's *The Revolution Betrayed* (1937). To use this shopworn frame of reference would have reduced a play to allegory and precluded any possibility that worldwide audiences might abstract from the fable, that they might distill the conflicts of the piece without prejudgment. A seventeenth-century setting allowed Brecht greater freedom in molding his material. ⟨. . .⟩

Brecht's strategy of composition in the play is to interlace moments of authentic seventeenth-century history with anachronisms and invented history to create a consistent set of parallels between two epochs. ⟨. . .⟩

The play depicts some twenty-five years of Galileo's life. In January 1610 he provided the foundations for scientific truth concerning the permanent revolution of the earth by proving Copernicus's theory and disproving the generally accepted Ptolemaic theory of earthly stasis. For the balance of his life Galileo maneuvered with the church hierarchy to gain recognition for his arguments. Ever insistent that he was a loyal child of the church, he became increasingly subservient and often unaccountably reticent in expressing his deepest convictions. With the death of the old pope, a new, scientifically trained man ascended the papal throne. This old acquaintance disappointed Galileo, put him on trial, convicted him, and finally humiliated him with enforced exile.

The parallels run like a red thread through the play. In January 1910—three centuries later to the month and year—Trotsky provided the scientific arguments concerning the permanent revolution of society in his Vienna "Truth," *Pravda,* and thus disproved the generally accepted theory that revolution must erupt in industrialized countries rather than agrarian lands. He further contended that Russia would spearhead revolution in the twentieth century. The middle segment of Galileo's life in the play (scenes 4–8) parallels Trotsky's struggle to gain recognition for his theories in the Bolshevik hierarchy, his submission to the Party and increasing subservience during the First World War, and the eight years of Lenin's leadership in the Soviet Union. Brecht altered the historical date of the old pope's death (i.e. the ascension of the new pope Barberini) from 1623 to 1624. The year 1924 saw Lenin's death and the ascension of Joseph Stalin, the man often referred to as the "red pope" or the Barbarian. Though he was trained in the science of Marxism, Stalin took control of the Party hierarchy, put the loyal child of the Party on trial, defeated him, and finally humiliated Trotsky with enforced exile. As in the seventeenth century when the Ptolemaic theory of the universe was upheld against the Copernican by way of force, the theory of "socialism in one land" was upheld by way of force in the twentieth century against the theory of permanent revolution. ⟨. . .⟩

Brecht's *Galileo* marked the beginning of a series of theatrical learning plays about the most significant stages in the effort to revolutionize feudal Russia. In *Galileo* Brecht had explored the questions of guilt and self-sacrifice, vital questions for the Left during the year in which he wrote the play. Moving from current events to recent history in *Mother Courage and Her Children*, he again treated the topic of party history: here during civil war. In *The Good Woman of Szechwan* he presented the difficulties of modernizing and industrializing in an underdeveloped land. Finally, in *The Caucasian Chalk Circle*, he probed party history and the saga of the grandiose revolutionary year 1917. Viewing revolutionary history from the perspective of the late 1930s made each earlier stage seem less complex, less difficult, with the battle lines more clearly delineated. This experience is reflected in the style and mood of the plays which progress from document to legend.

—Betty N. Weber, "The Life of Galileo and the Theory of Revolution in Permanence," *Bertolt Brecht: Political Theory and Literary Practice.* Ed. by Betty N. Weber and Hubert Heinen (Athens: The University of Georgia Press, 1980): pp. 62–64, 75.

GUY STERN ON THE HIDDEN THEME OF EXILE

[Guy Stern is a professor of German at Wayne. His work is mainly on the Enlightenment and literature of exile, with a focus on German cultural history. He has written on Brecht, Kurt Weill, and the Weimar times.]

Four aspects of the exile experience permeate the drama: the flight, economic straits, loss of identity, and intellectual suppression of the refugees. Flight, the necessity of "changing one's country more often than one's shoes," had become a way of life to Brecht; even his departure from the United States resembled one. It is therefore understandable that Brecht has his hero prepare for flight as prudently as did Brecht at various stages of his exile. ⟨. . .⟩

Brecht's flight from Germany brought him freedom coupled with deprivation; this was typical of the fate of the refugee. ⟨. . .⟩

Brecht, ⟨. . .⟩ throughout the drama, shows that even this vaunted freedom is not unalloyed—and that it is particularly precarious for foreigners. To make his point, Brecht has his protagonist recall the fate of Giordano Bruno, who was delivered up to the Inquisition by the Republic of Florence, the supposed protector of freedom. In trying to exculpate his government, the curator cites the historic "party line," that Bruno was extradited not for his heresies, but because he was a foreigner: ⟨. . .⟩.

This argument is unconvincing from the start. It is furthermore demolished completely by subsequent speeches and also fails in its purpose to assuage the fears of Galileo. Hence its function within the play is difficult to fathom. But it makes perfect sense as a topical reference. ⟨. . .⟩

⟨. . .⟩ Brecht's use of dates referring to historical events in the seventeenth century, which are not absolutely essential to the drama of Galileo, tends to emphasize the parallelism. Dates such as 1633 and 1637 evoke the memory of events precisely 300 years later. They also evoke parallelism between the life of Brecht as an exile and that of Galileo as an intellectual exile—choosing the seventeenth-century equivalent of "inner emigration." Occasionally Brecht attributed his persecution by the Nazis in part to the Marxist tenor of his didactic plays: "Then [Mr. Brecht] . . . asked you too often where the riches of the rich come from / And right off you abruptly chased him out of the country" (verse added to the "Salomonlied").

The year 1932 falls into this specific period of Brecht's creativity with the completion of such works as *Die Mutter* [*The Mother*] and *Kuhle Wampe*. Brecht appears to imply that one of the factors that led to the silencing or intellectual exile of Galileo was the application of his teachings to the socioeconomic and political arena. In fact, scene 10 in *Galileo Galilei* is a didactic play in a nutshell proceeding from the observation of a neutral scientific fact, the earth revolving around the sun, to a utopia of the class struggle in which the master is a satellite of his servants. Brecht as the embattled and endangered writer of didactic plays joins hands across several centuries with Galileo Galilei, who inspired didactic satire, the Shrovetide Plays. ⟨. . .⟩

The next year, or so Brecht seems to argue, both he and Galileo pay the price for carrying abstract insights to their logical conclusion. The forces that compel Brecht's involuntary emigration, "When I Was Driven into Exile," drove Galileo into his intellectual exile. With one spatial reference that consciously or subconsciously reinforces the temporal one, Brecht drives home the parallel. In '33 both Brecht and Galileo started a prolonged residence in a *Landhaus* ("country house"). ⟨. . .⟩ Galileo becomes Brecht's "legendary" alter ego. ⟨. . .⟩

The discovery of this particular hidden theme in Brecht's *Galileo* may, beyond its pertinence for Brecht scholarship, help solve a problem of classification in modern German literature. One of the earlier books on exile literature suggests that we will arrive at a valid typology of the genre only if we discover traces of the exile experience in works thematically divorced from it. In *Galileo* we have a striking example of such a transplanted exile landscape.

> —Guy Stern, "The Plight of the Exile: A Hidden Theme in Brecht's *Galileo Galilei," Exile: The Writer's Experience.* Ed. by John M. Spalek and Robert F. Bell (Chapel Hill: The University of North Carolina Press, 1982): pp. 133–38.

Doc Rossi on *Hamlet* and *Galileo*

[Doc Rossi has taught English and American Literature at the undergraduate level in London and Rome. He has published works on Shakespeare and Brecht, the Beat Generation, Scott Fitzgerald, and Thomas Pynchon.]

There are some striking connections between these two plays: both exist in three "authoritative" texts, each version quite different from the others, the final version being perhaps too long for production. ⟨. . .⟩

Brecht's writings on *Hamlet,* as with nearly all his work concerning Shakespeare, consist mostly of fragmentary pieces scattered across a broad range of forms in many contexts, but his understanding of the play focuses, as in his sonnet, on the decision Hamlet must make given what he does and does not know. After attending a Swedish production of *Hamlet* on 20 November 1940, Brecht noted in his journal the inadequacy of productions that emphasize "the representation of the vacillating and hesitating intellectual man," that render Hamlet "simply an idealist who is thrown off the rails by the violent clash with the real world, the idealist who becomes a cynic." According to Brecht's reading of the play, it is "not a question of acting or not acting, . . . rather the question is to remain silent or not to remain silent, to approve or not to approve," an attitude influenced by Hitler's aggressions in Europe. In other words, the problem is not a particular action itself but the motivation behind that action. ⟨. . .⟩

⟨T⟩he rise of the Nazi party informs Brecht's reading and makes it necessary for him to portray Hamlet's predicament as deadly: the prince's lack of commitment denies action until it is too late. This concern for committed action which predates the *Reichstag* fire and Brecht's subsequent flight from Germany shows up most clearly perhaps in *The Measures Taken* (1929–30); it also seems to have played an important part in Brecht's 1931 adaptation of *Hamlet*. ⟨. . .⟩

According to Brecht, in *Hamlet* suggestion or suspicion sets off a process of interpretation which is always in danger of becoming circular, of reaching self-verifying conclusions unless one uses a method of interpretation similar to Montaigne's or the new scientific method of Bacon. ⟨. . .⟩

Brecht's concern with the representation of the Ghost in *Hamlet* suggests a way of understanding the play in relation to his "theater for the scientific age" and his working out of ideas associated with it in *Galileo*. In the *Arbeitsjournal* entry concerning the Swedish production of *Hamlet*, Brecht describes Shakespeare's stage practice as "surrealistic, although admittedly without the shock effect for which surrealism aims, it is an innocent surrealism (For instance the field headquarters of two hostile armies on one stage simultaneously)." ⟨. . .⟩

Brecht's dramaturgical practice in *Galileo* presents critical thinking as the object as well as the subject of the play. Like Shakespeare, Brecht is writing neither biography nor history per se—nor is he writing political propaganda, although his technique has political significance—but a work which demonstrates historical significance both in its content and in the way it represents the production of history. Brecht's alteration of historical fact, his rewriting of history to suit his own purposes—e.g. "The truth about the telescope" supposedly revealed in scene 2—demonstrates how subjective distortions are assimilated and accepted as fact. By historicizing fiction Brecht demonstrates how history is fictionalized; he portrays it as an arranged, interpreted account of facts similar to Galileo's proofs. The narrative perspective of *Galileo* is characterized by its skeptical, austere materialism, its debunking of the mysterious and of the idealist point of view, while its structure shows the fracture points between these opposing perspectives. ⟨. . .⟩

Like Hamlet, Galileo feels that with time he can organize the "wretched odds and ends" of his proofs into irrefutable truth and pins his hopes on the power reason has over people like the sea captain, who allows for storms and doldrums when laying in stores, and other practical-minded people such as Mrs. Sarti and the Little Monk. But as the play progresses it becomes evident that Galileo is completely unprepared for the (to him) irrational behavior of the authorities and their own appropriation of the truth. ⟨. . .⟩

Galileo's decision to go on the attack in order to force through the truth is similar to what Hamlet attempts with *The Murder of Gonzago*. The exchange between Andrea and the young Duke Cosimo at the beginning of scene 4 parallels much of scene 1. Andrea takes the part of Galileo, repeating his words ("This place is getting like a pigeon loft") and adopting his teacher's seemingly uncontrollable desire to teach and so spread the truth. But Andrea, reflecting Galileo's new determination, is less even-tempered with his student than Galileo had been with him. ⟨. . .⟩

The Shakespearean dramaturgy Brecht employs in his traditional drama (as opposed to that of the *Lehrstücke*) juxtaposes the "reality" represented in *The Measures Taken* with other perspectives and exposes the limitations of each. In *Galileo*, the revolutionary content of the *Lehrstücke* is represented in what Brecht calls a reactionary form, and this goes further than making the content more palatable, more suitable for consumption in the culinary theater: it exposes the content to dialectical criticism by revealing paradoxes and contradictions without demonstrating solutions. The commitment to representing change—and in Brecht's case to a dialectical drama perpetuated by a critical skepticism affecting both form and content—can only explore, examine, and interrogate; it cannot prove. ⟨. . .⟩

When Brecht had finished *Galileo* in January of 1939, he had copies run off and sent one to his old friend Walter Benjamin. After reading it, Benjamin commented that the "hero" of the work is not Galileo at all but the people. Brecht valued Benjamin's remark but found it "too briefly expressed," and added that the play "shows how society extorts from its individuals what it needs from them." Thus Galileo "raises his telescope to the stars and delivers himself to the rack," while the Church, "with all its forces of reaction . . . [is] able to bring off an organized retreat and more or less reassert its power." Hamlet, elevating individual reason above traditional authorities, delivers himself to the sword and leaves all that has just passed to be interpreted from a military perspective supported by divine right. Both are criminals, but, as Brecht notes, "Confronted with such a situation, one can scarcely wish only to praise or only to condemn." When the bells of St. Mark's begin to toll—announcing to Galileo's faithful followers that something is rotten in the state of science, that Galileo has recanted under the convincing arguments of the Inquisition—Andrea proclaims in a loud voice "Unhappy the land that has no heroes!" to which the beleaguered Galileo answers, "No. Unhappy the land where heroes are needed," a fitting epitaph for both plays.

—Doc Rossi, "Hamlet and The Life of Galileo," *Comparative Drama* 32, no. 4 (Winter 1998–99): pp. 497–98, 500, 503–4, 509–11, 513, 515–16.

Plot Summary of
The Caucasian Chalk Circle
(Der Kaukasische Kreidekreis)

After *The Good Woman of Sezuan, The Caucasian Chalk Circle* is Brecht's best known parable play. It was written in 1944–1945 in California, in collaboration with Ruth Berlau, translated into English by Maja Apelman and Eric Bentley, and first performed in English in Northfield, Minnesota in 1947. The first German production took place in 1954 in Berlin. This late play is the most epic of Brecht's works. Its lines of action are highly stylized. It is composed of an extensive, challenging, and much debated prologue, as well as two major stories, whose two audiences are the farmers in the prologue as much as the spectators in the theater.

The prologue presents a debate about a piece of land. It introduces two Soviet collective farms in post-war Russia, whose farmers meet in 1945 after the liberation from the German occupation, in order to decide which farm should have the land of the valley for cultivation. Before the war, the valley belonged to the goat-breeding farm Kolkhoz Galinsk, but meanwhile, the neighboring Kolkhoz Rosa Luxemburg, which specializes in growing fruit and producing wine, planned an impeccable irrigation system and ends up with the piece of land, for it makes most sense to render the valley most productive. In order for both groups of farmers to understand the basis of this judgment, they are told two illustrating and somewhat parallel stories, which constitute the main corpus of the piece.

The actual play is a double flashback. It is set in the past and delivered as two stories, maid Grusha's and scribe Azdak's, which are entirely separate at first, but end up merging in the sixth and final trial scene. The main story begins as a narration. *In olden times, in bloody times* Georgi Abaschwili was Governor in feudal Georgia and lived there with his family. One day princes began to revolt against the Grand Duke, and prince Arsen Kazbeki ordered the Governor's execution. Abaschwili was murdered and his frightened wife Natella fled, leaving the baby son Michael behind. Grusha Vachnadze, a kitchen maid, rescued the child by taking it with her to the mountains, where her brother Lavrenti Vachnadze lived with his wife. In her motherly altruism, Grusha even consented to then marry a rich, old and sick peasant by name of Yussup, solely to give the child a name and a home.

To Grusha's dismay, dying Yussup revived. He had only pretended his illness in order not to have to fight in the war. But now the war was over. Grusha's fiancé Simon Chachava returned from service and found her married with a child. And soldiers promptly seized the boy, for Natella Abaschwili, the former Governor's wife and Michael's biological mother, sued for his return home. Therefore, Grusha and Natella were to meet in court. To be able to really understand the subsequent trial, one needs to find out more about Azdak. And Brecht makes Azdak's story available to us in scenes four and five. It is a story parallel to Grusha's of scenes two and three, and it takes us back to the time of the revolt—a narrative technique which enables Brecht to trace the disreputable career of rogue, clerk, and judge Azdak.

When the Governor was murdered, Azdak, then a drunken village rogue and scribe, gave shelter to a beggar, who then turned out to be the Grand Duke. Azdak felt that having saved this ruthless creature's skin was an unforgivable crime, so that he asked the constable for the man's arrest in order to then take him to court. But in the troubled city the last judge had just been hanged. A group of rebellious soldiers was so thrilled by Azdak's amusing endeavors that they promptly and arbitrarily appointed him judge. As a consequence, Azdak was judging the people for two years. Generally, he was corrupt and without scruples, and occasionally he favored the poor.

When Grusha and then Natella appear before Azdak in court, he too is about to be hanged, but then the Grand Duke's unlikely messenger rushes in with good news. The Duke wants to promptly appoint the man who saved his life to be judge over the city. Already on location, Azdak then listens to Grusha's and Natella's pleas, draws a chalk circle on the ground and puts Michael in the middle. Each woman is supposed to drag the child out of the center, thereby proving her strong motherly will. Natella violently pulls the poor boy out of the circle, while Grusha gently lets him go, unable to bear the sight of the traditional tugging. Judge Azdak grants custody to Grusha, for her tenderness most obviously demonstrates a true mother's love for the boy. Moreover, Azdak chases Natella away and awards Grusha with a divorce from her husband Yussup, so that she can finally return to her fiancé Simon Chachava.

After settling the case, Azdak disappears into anonymity, while the singer rounds off the story with an interpretative reading of it, merging prologue and main play by the following morale: things should belong to those who are good for them, to those who serve them best, not to those who want to possess them; children to the truly motherly, and valleys to those who most productively render them fruitful. What then is the function of the prologue and why does it not constitute the whole play, given that the morale could be entirely drawn from the situation depicted in it? Why is the play entitled *The Caucasian Chalk Circle*, if the chalk circle episode only makes up one scene? What is the rest of the play there for?

It is significant that Brecht rearranged Li Hsing Tao's 13th-century Chinese parable of the chalk circle, which Klabund had adapted into German in the 1920's. In the Chinese legend, the judge is able to discriminate the biological mother from the want-to-be mother because out of fear of hurting the child, the biological mother does not pull him. Brecht transforms this setting and gives the child to the one who is not the biological mother, and does so in a case where the biological mother is, so to speak, not a mother. Natella's selfish possessiveness alone cannot qualify, if the more motherly foster mother Grusha is by far more likely to bring up Michael in a way that makes him a better person and community member. In Brecht, the chalk circle test is a legal procedure that helps to clarify, convict and set free, but it is also a measure that calls for criticism. ❀

List of Characters in
The Caucasian Chalk Circle

Georgi Abaschwili, the governor, is beheaded after his brother the Fat Prince successfully stages a coup.

Natella Abaschwili, Georgi's wife who leaves her son Michael behind when she flees the Fat Prince. She later tries to get Michael back in order to reclaim the Governor's estates.

Michael Abaschwili, the governor's son, is raised by Grusha after his mother abandons him. Grusha later claims him as her own child and Azdak, the judge, allows her to keep him.

Simon Chachava, a soldier loyal to the Grand Duke. Grusha promises to marry him when he returns from the war, but marries Yussup instead. This marriage is eventually annulled, allowing Grusha and Simon to reunite.

Grusha Vachnadze, is a kitchen maid in the palace. She rescues the Governor's son Michael and takes him with her. She cares for the child for two years until Natella reclaims Michael. Both women are forced to appear before Azdak who chooses to give the boy to Grusha.

Lavrenti Vachnadze, Grusha's brother, with whom she stays for an entire winter. He finally gets rid of his sister by making her marry a "dying" man, Jessup.

Aniko, Lavrenti's wife and Grusha's sister-in-law, described as a religious woman. She desperately tries to get Grusha out of her house.

Yussup, the "dying" man Grusha is forced to marry in order to keep Michael.

Arsen Kazbeki, the fat prince. He is the brother of the Governor, and he stages a coup in which he kills his brother. After ruling for two years he is deposed and beheaded by the return of the Grand Duke.

Azdak, the village scribe who accidentally saves the Grand Duke's life. He is later made a judge and rules in Grusha's favor.

Shauva, a policeman. He becomes Azdak's assistant after Azdak becomes judge. ❀

Critical Views on
The Caucasian Chalk Circle

RONALD GRAY ON NATURE AND OPPOSITION

[Ronald Gray's books include *Bertolt Brecht, Brecht the Dramatist, Franz Kafka, Goethe: A Critical Introduction,* and *Introduction to German Poetry.*]

The scenes of Grusha's escape, adventures, marriage and rejection by Simon, forming about half the play, make a loosely strung narrative in the fashion of "epic" theater. While there is a certain thread connecting them, however—they do not stand "each for themselves," as Brecht suggested earlier that "epic" scenes should do—the interest is sustained not so much by the thin plot as by the detailed interactions of the characters and by the beauty of the portrayal. Since *Baal,* Brecht had scarcely made any use in his plays of the natural scene. In *The Caucasian Chalk Circle,* as in *Puntila* and *The Good Woman* and in his later poetry, the world of nature returns. The scene by the river itself, indicated on the stage merely by two ground-rows of reeds, evokes by its bareness, coupled with the lyrical song of the narrator preceding it, an awareness of loveliness. The icicles above Grusha's hut, as she waits in isolation for the winter to pass, become moving tokens of spring as they melt, and the musical notes of a xylophone offstage, recording the falling drops of water, add excitement by their rising intensity. There is time for contemplation and for exhilaration in these austerely presented moments; the spectator is not whirled along as he was by the action of earlier plays, and not encouraged to indulge in ecstatic Nature worship, but rather to recognize with pleasure the delight that is to be had from Nature, off the stage. There is both detachment and attachment.

The settings also, in this part of the play, evoke an astringent delight. The descending white back cloth has already been mentioned. There is also the scene of Grusha's wedding, contrived to give a Breughelesque harmony of brown, oatmeal, sepia, and an occasional splash of red: peasant colors in a peasant setting, crowded, earthy, vulgarly frank, but shaped into a frame of unity that is comic, sympathetic, and has a lopsided symmetry of its own. There is the strange effect of the empty stage after the insurrection has passed by, with the voice of the narrator emerging from one side to comment on the silence and thereby, oddly enough, to intensify it. Meanwhile, from time to time, the prose speech breaks into verse such as that in which Grusha affirms her love at Simon's first departure:

> Simon Chachava, I will wait for you.
> Go in good heart to the battle, soldier,
> The bloody battle, the bitter battle
> From which not all come back:
> When you come back, I will be there.
> I will wait for you under the green elm
> I will wait for you under the bare elm
> I will wait till the last man comes back
> And longer . . .

It comes as a shock to go on from this moving language and these scenes to the following series which forgets Grusha entirely in order to introduce the story of the judge Azdak. From Azdak's first speech, the spectator is hit by a forceful language which English can barely reproduce: "Schnaub nicht, du bist kein Gaul. Und es hilft dir nicht bei der Polizei, wenn du läufst, wie ein Rotz im April. Steh, sag ich. . . . Setz dich nieder und futtre, da ist ein Stück Käse. Lang nichts gefressen? Warum bist du gerannt, du Arschloch?" The crudity of this, the rough vigor, the cynicism and humor and the underlying sympathy introduce the character of Azdak himself, which stands in strange contrast to Grusha's. Azdak is a thief, a timeserver, a coward, who by a lucky accident is raised during the insurrection to a position of authority. As a judge he is corrupt, licentious, contemptuous of law and order, a lickspittle. His life is spent, unlike Grusha's, not in rebellious opposition to society's moral standards, but in careful adaptation to them, going along with the tide, and keeping an eye on the main chance. But such an account does less than justice to this unpredictable rogue. ⟨. . .⟩

Azdak is a standing affront, and at the same time a standing reminder of the questionable values on which society is based. He has one principle, that the rights of the poor are disregarded and that this situation must be reversed. Apart from that, he proceeds *ad hoc.* ⟨. . .⟩

In the final scene of all, the two sides are confronted with one another, the disruptive, ambiguous underminer and the calm, shrewd, motherly girl who would rather die than forego her humanity. Azdak is called to try the case in which the real mother of Grusha's "child," the wife of the former governor of the province, claims possession of her son. ⟨. . .⟩ Azdak proceeds, however, as usual, accepting bribes from the wealthier party, while abusing Simon and Grusha who have nothing to offer him, and it is this which brings on the first serious opposition he has had to encounter. Grusha declares that she has no respect for a judge such as he is, "no more than I have for a thief and a murderer that does what he likes." Her moral protest is a straightforward indictment of his libertinism (which is no mere show), and none the worse for that; in fact she has all, or nearly all, our sympathy. Yet the end will have already been guessed. After the "trial of the chalk circle" in which each woman is to pull at the child from different sides, and Grusha fails to pull for fear of hurting the boy, Azdak ceremonially declares that Grusha is the true mother since she alone has shown true motherly feelings. This is not, however, a sentimental ending awarding victory to justice against the run of the odds. Rather, it is the fusion of two conceptions of justice. Azdak's instinctive prompting on this occasion (he is, after all, in safety now, with the governor's wife in political disgrace) is to award Grusha the custody of the child. But this instinctive prompting is a part of his elemental originality, his closeness to the roots of his nature, and his complete detachment from them. His decision has gathered the weight and incontrovertibility of a natural phenomenon, and despite his mockery of the virtues here is one virtue in Grusha that he respects without thought of argument. ⟨. . .⟩

Thus the two sides come together.

—Ronald Gray, "On Brecht's *The Caucasian Chalk Circle*," *Brecht: A Collection of Critical Essays*. Ed. by Peter Demetz (Englewood Cliffs, N. J.: Prentice-Hall Inc., 1962): pp. 152–56.

Maria P. Alter on the Technique of Alienation

[In addition to Maria Alter's writings on Brecht, she has written on Hans Carossa and Arthur Schnitzler.]

The concept of alienation may be broken down into a purpose, which affects mainly the general impact of the play, and a certain number of technical devices used to achieve this purpose. The purpose, which connects alienation to the general theory of the "epic theater," is to develop the political awareness of the audience, to teach while entertaining, and to force the spectators to draw concrete (and preferably revolutionary) conclusions from the issues presented on the stage. The alienation thus establishes a special relation between the audience and the play, whereby the former views the latter as an object lesson. ⟨. . .⟩

The action of the play takes place in a half-imaginary, exotic setting (for the Western audience, the Russian province of Georgia is indeed a legendary land); it is supernatural in some aspects; and it tells a tale specifically designed to yield a lesson. In fact, the final and key scene refers directly to one of Solomon's sentences (as well as to a similar conclusion in an old Chinese play). ⟨. . .⟩

The technical devices of alienation serve the main purpose by establishing a distance between the audience and the play, so that the spectators may be constantly reminded that they are viewing a play (hence an object lesson) and not a real event. In that sense, alienation is the very opposite of the technique of illusion which has been traditionally employed on the Western stage, where the main aim of the playwright was always to draw the spectator into the world created in the play, cause him to identify with the heroes, and live emotionally the theatrical experience for the sake of catharsis. Brecht, on the contrary, tries to break the magic of the theater and to startle periodically the spectator into realization that he is attending only a performance, looking at actors, witnessing parables from which he should draw dispassionate conclusions.

Viewed in this perspective, *The Caucasian Chalk Circle* shows clearly that Brecht does not make any attempt at realism or any illusion of reality. The feeling of unreality is first created not only by the prologue, discussed above, but especially by the way in which that prologue introduces *The Caucasian Chalk Circle* proper as merely a play within a play. ⟨. . .⟩ The same effect is obtained through the presence of musicians on the stage, and the use of some characters from the prologue as the chorus in the body of the play. In addition, Brecht indicates that the story-teller must appear with a book, which he is supposed to consult from time to time. Obviously, each time the spectators see him turning a page, they remember the literary and artificial character of the spectacle, and realize anew that they attend a parable.

Alienation devices abound also in the text of the play. Its construction testifies to a search for discontinuous impressions, throwing the spectator in and out of the main stream of action. This sensation is achieved especially by the songs, which interrupt the flow of scenes and often have no relation whatever to the story. ⟨. . .⟩ This disruption of movement is also brought about by the succession of different moods, as *The Caucasian Chalk Circle* moves back and forth between comedy, violence, fantasy, terror, irony, pity, poetic love, with a rapidity that leaves no time for adjustment. The versatile function of the chorus contributes to the same end. As in the Greek drama, it comments on the action, summarizes the problems, and underscores the ideas of the play. In addition, however, it substitutes occasionally for the characters of the play and tells what they are thinking while they remain silent on the stage. As a result, the audience is forced to shift its perspective, and suddenly finds itself on the sidelines, after having been immersed in the action: the distance between the spectators and the actors becomes more pronounced through this interposition of the chorus. ⟨. . .⟩

Other alienation effects stem from the impact of Brecht's ironical paradoxes and belong to the content rather than the structure of the play. They bring about the kind of surprise which breaks the emotional spell of the action.

—Maria P. Alter, "The Technique of Alienation in Bertolt Brecht's *The Caucasian Chalk Circle*," *The College Language Association Journal* 8, no. 1 (September 1964): pp. 60–63.

[Helen Whall received her Ph.D. from Yale in 1976 and has since been teaching at the College of the Holy Cross. She has written on Tudor Drama.]

Consider the juxtapositions which Brecht has arranged: The Prologue depicts, as Thomas Whitaker notes, "some proletarian pastoral in the 1945 of a future that never was." Grusha's story—the first song, second play—is a romance adventure in which the heroine flees a corrupt court and, as a result, is separated from the man she loves. She takes with her a child whom she will learn to love. To protect the child, she will marry a man whom she knows she cannot love. The army pursues and captures her. Azdak's story—second song, third play—is, as Bentley points out, a Saturnalia—a play of inversions heavy with ironic potential.

What happens between these modular units of comedy is important to what happens within each. The Prologue seems to end quickly and leads directly to Grusha's story. But the conclusion to Grusha's story is held in suspense. The Pastoral Prologue—we readily identify Brecht's idealized peasants as inhabitants of the pastoral world—had fulfilled our expectations of pastoral conventions. By holding back the conclusion to Grusha's story, itself so clearly based upon the formulas of adventure-romance, Brecht tempts us to predict the outcome of her story by once again trusting to traditional solutions. But the conventions of romance lead us to two conclusions: the tragic and the comedic; separation or marriage. ⟨. . .⟩

The process of Brecht's total play, *The Caucasian Chalk Circle*, is then neither tragic linear development nor even satiric inversion. Satire never touches Grusha. Her goodness is goodness no matter which way it is turned. Rather, the process of Brecht's play is that of comedic circularity. We complete the satiric process of Azdak's story and return immediately to the opening of the play in order to conclude the now integrated drama. The total play is, finally, a pastoral, just as is the Prologue—though not in the same manner. The traditional pastoral mode may seem too simple for modern man, who admires complexity of form as well as ambiguity of content; indeed, many contemporary directors have cut Brecht's Prologue in dread of its simplicity, fearing that the Prologue either makes socialism seem too attractive for the tastes of a capitalist audience or concerned that it reduces socialism to a simplistic answer—"reason should rule." Such thinking ignores the complexity of thought behind the formal simplicity of pastoral art, an art which has always been the product of and brought pleasure to extremely sophisticated men. Brecht both recognizes this complexity and grasps modern insensitivity to the form. He rescues the pastoral tradition by wedding his simple pastoral prologue to more accessible complex forms. He alters not the pastoral conventions—honest rustics, in harmony with nature, reach truth through rational debate—but the context in which we now reconsider those conventions. Thus, when we reach the conclusion of Grusha's story, we return to the simple blunt lesson of the opening pastoral—reason should rule—and realize that reason is not an answer, not an ending, but an activity, a process, a process much like the movement of Brecht's play, an activity in which we ourselves have engaged while viewing this play and which has led to the play's happy conclusion. The Prologue can neither be cut nor considered alone. To do either is not only to deny, but to destroy the integrity of the play, for to separate the Prologue is to cut the complex geometry of Brecht's clean circle. 〈. . .〉

Brecht's triumph as a modern artist comes in rescuing the pastoral world itself from the same tradition of nostalgia. His concern is with new beginnings, not old endings. His pastoral world *is* in some future—not one that wasn't, but one that hasn't yet been chosen. The pastoral tradition, made new, provides the third plot of Brecht's play; this singular use of the number three constitutes a significant choice on the artist's part to break from the series of balanced doubles we see within the play. Only in retrospect, however, can we realize that the initial story of the Causasian peasants is both true beginning, middle, and end of the total play. This is the Caucasian chalk circle. 〈. . .〉

We leave the theater not with our lost dream world of hierarchy and degree reestablished for us, as is the method of older pastorals, but in search of a new beginning that may allow for the future we glimpsed at the beginning of a play. And Brecht, through a bit of theft, some sleight of hand and a great deal of genius, manages to resolve in art conflicts which may—or may not—be resolvable in life.

—Helen M. Whall, "Future Perfect: The Pastoral Tense of Bertolt Brecht's *The Caucasian Chalk Circle*," *Studies in the Humanities* 9, no. 1 (December 1981): pp. 12–15.

[Maria Shevtsova is professor of drama at Goldsmiths College at the University of London. Her stress on performance analysis and tendency toward interdisciplinarity opened up a new international outlook on the theater. She is the author of numerous articles and books, among them *Theatre and Cultural Interaction*, as well as the editor of focus issues of the *Contemporary Theatre Review* and *Theatre Research International*.]

Written between 1941 and 1944 during Brecht's exile in the United States, *The Caucasian Chalk Circle* is made up of two stories, Grusha's, which starts in Scene 2, and Azdak's, which does not begin until Scene 5, the penultimate scene of the play. ⟨. . .⟩

Disagreement over the play's structure and its implications for the meaning of the whole is an inevitable consequence of Azdak's arriving so late in the piece. By this time Grusha's story has almost run its course. ⟨. . .⟩

What the plot sets up, in fact, is a social dynamic between the numerous figures that appear and drop out of sight. Consequently, instead of simply displaying relationships between individuals, each group of figures is animated by the interaction between social classes that constitutes social relations as such. In other words, as is typical of Brecht's corpus, encounters between individuals are informed by the interests, habits, assumptions and aspirations pertinent to the class, or social group within a given class, to which the individuals interacting with each other belong. In this way, Brecht shows that what may be thought to be a purely individual action is social through and through. The social relations presented in *The Caucasian Chalk Circle* are not considered to be generically 'human' and, therefore, true for all time. They are embedded in the specific conditions of war ⟨. . .⟩.

The social dynamic of Grusha's story does not rely on inward-looking, psychologically detailed explanations for this or that motive or this or that outcome. Everything is communicated outwardly, through what happens when it happens rather than through states of mind and soul. And this is precisely why Brecht, when mounting *The Caucasian Chalk Circle* with the Berliner Ensemble in 1954, used his theatre's turntable stage to such great advantage by having all changes of setting during Grusha's journey through the mountains come towards her. The changing landscape highlighted the main events of the narrative; and, of course, events in any story involve the actions of protagonists. The motion of space in time (the passage of time being suggested on stage, as in the text, through narrative sequence) allowed the spectators' gaze to fix on the external conditions that gave rise to, and accounted for, not only Grusha's but everybody else's actions, all of them demonstrating something about each other. ⟨...⟩

⟨T⟩he theme of war is quite pronounced throughout, acting as a linking device between the relatively wide range of events taking place. ⟨...⟩

The war trial concludes with yet another contradiction when Azdak the rascal is made a judge. ⟨...⟩

⟨T⟩he themes of war and justice are brought together. From here on, Grusha and Azdak's combined story rapidly comes to a close. The chalk test is carried out twice. Grusha refuses both times to pull Michael out of the circle because she cannot bear to hurt the child that she has raised. She proves by her action that the true mother is the caring mother, and so gets the child. Azdak divorces her from the peasant she has married. She is now free to marry Simon. Natella loses her estates. The city gains a garden for children. Justice is done for the just. The unjust are undone. Even so, the play does not close on an unqualified happy ending. The feudal order of the Grand Duke is restored. Grusha and Simon have to leave town. Azdak, the harbinger of social change, disappears, never to be heard of again except in legends and folk-tales—or in Brecht's theatre.

What, then, is to be made of the epilogue/moral of the story that confirms Azdak's judgement? The moral is: 'That what there is shall belong to those who are good for it, thus / The children to the maternal, that they may thrive; / The carriages to good drivers, that they are driven well; / And the valley to the waterers, that it shall bear fruit.' The reference here to the waterers of the valley recalls Scene I which is like a prologue to *The Caucasian Chalk Circle*. The scene tells of a dispute between two collective farms in Georgia shortly after the Second World War. One group of peasants wishes to resettle the valley where they had previously produced excellent goat's cheese. They had moved their goat-herds, albeit on advice from the authorities, at the approach of Hitler's armies. By doing so they effectively abandoned the land to the enemy. The other group wishes to irrigate the valley for orchards and vineyards. Its members are partisans who defended the valley against the Nazi invasion. The problem is amicably solved, the valley going to those who had fought and suffered for it and would nurture the land and, literally, make it grow. It is, of course, significant that life-giving water will be brought to the land. The performance prepared for the occasion is 'The Chalk Circle', a Chinese legend revised to fit a chapter of Georgia's medieval history and which, the guests are told, bears on the problem at hand.

Now, such a legend actually exists. Brecht uses it in conjunction with folk-tale elements from the European tradition (quests, journeys, obstacles that must be surmounted, chance events that prove to have been there by design, 'magical' solutions, and other folk-tale qualities permeating the play). And he uses the legend to give the prologue, the core of the work (which is the play within the play connecting Grusha and Azdak's stories) and the very short epilogue summing up the proceedings, the aura as well as the authority of folk-wisdom. The prologue is a framing device. But its tale of the valley is analogous with Grusha's tale which, as we have seen, fits into Azdak's. The structure is that of Chinese boxes (or Russian dolls?). The epilogue/moral draws its full sense and meaning from this interlocking structure.

Furthermore, although Brecht adapted the Chinese legend to suit his purposes (in the legend, for example, the biological mother is the nurturing mother), he appears to have kept the general drift of its moral and philosophical argument. Just the same, he gave it a new dimension by transposing the argument to a war context. This meant that the argument now had quite a different resonance, its reach going well beyond the area covered in the original. The war context at issue is not confined to old Grusinia, Brecht's fantasy name for Georgia. It incorporates modern Europe. ⟨...⟩

In the light of Brecht's acute awareness of events and debates in Europe while he still lived there, whether in Germany, or later in exile in Denmark, Sweden and Finland, it would be perfectly appropriate to assume that he kept his ear to the ground (and to the radio) for information on Europe during his exile in the United States.

News was all the more likely to have crossed the Atlantic because of America's forestalled, but nevertheless anticipated, entry into the war. Apart from such factors beyond Brecht's control, there was the control he exercised in respect of his own political choices. Politics was the driving force behind Brecht's exile in America. And exile is bound to have sharpened his perception of Europe.

—Maria Shevtsova, "*The Caucasian Chalk Circle:* The View from Europe," *The Cambridge Companion to Brecht.* Ed. by Peter Thomson and Glendyr Sacks (Cambridge: Cambridge University Press, 1994): pp. 153, 155–58, 160–63.

Works by
Bertolt Brecht

Bertolt Brecht and his collaborators wrote more than thirty plays, about one hundred and fifty prose texts (not counting diaries or letters), roughly one thousand and three hundred poems and songs, numerous fragments, and three novels. Therefore, the following list cannot be more than selection.

The Beggar or the Dead Dog. 1919.

He Exorcizes a Devil. 1919.

Lux in Tenebris. 1919.

Baal. 1919.

Drums in the Night. 1922.

In the Jungle of the Cities. 1923.

Life of Edward II of England. 1923.

Man Is Man. 1925.

The Baby Elephant. 1925.

Bertolt Brecht's Domestic Breviary. 1927.

Mahagonny. 1927.

The Threepenny Opera. 1928.

Happy End. 1928.

The Flight of the Lindberghs. 1928.

Rise and Fall of the City of Mahagonny. 1929.

Didactic Play of Baden on Consent. 1929.

The Measures Taken. 1930.

He Who Said Yes, He Who Said No. 1930.

The Bread Shop. 1930.

Meditations of Herr Keuner. 1930–1957.

Saint Joan of the Stockyards. 1930.

The Mother. 1932.

The Seven Deadly Sins. 1933.

The Threepenny Novel. 1934.

Round Heads and Pointed Heads. 1934.

The Horatians and the Curiatians. 1936.

Señora Carrar's Rifles. 1937.

The Messingkauf Dialogues. 1937–1951.

The Exception and the Rule. 1938.

The Good Woman of Sezuan. 1938–1940.

Svendborg Poems. 1939.

Mother Courage and Her Children. 1939.

The Resistible Rise of Arturo Ui. 1941.

Galileo. 1943, 1947, 1957.

The Caucasian Chalk Circle. 1944–1945.

Fear and Misery in the Third Reich. 1945.

Herr Puntila and His Servant Matti. 1948.

Little Organon for the Theater. 1948.

Tales from the Calendar. 1949.

The Trial of Lucullus. 1949–1950.

The Private Tutor. 1950.

Coriolanus. 1953.

Buchow Elegies. 1953.

The Days of the Commune. 1956.

The Business Deals of Mr. Julius Caesar. 1957.

Schweyk in the Second World War. 1957.

The Visions of Simone Marchard. 1961.

Me-Ti. Book of Twists and Turns. 1965.

The Tui-Novel. 1967.

Works About
Bertolt Brecht

Bentley, Eric. "Brecht, Poetry, Drama and the People." *The Nation*, 157 (31 July 1943): 130–131.

———. *The Brecht Commentaries 1943–1980*. New York: Grove Press, 1981.

———. *The Brecht Memoir*. New York: PAJ Publications, 1985.

———. *The Playwright as Thinker: A Study of Drama in Modern Times*. New York: Harcourt, Brace and World, 1967.

Berlin Ensemble. *Bertolt Brecht and the Berlin Ensemble*. Berlin: Society for Cultural Relations with Foreign Countries, 1958.

Brecht Heute-Brecht Today. Yearbook of the International Brecht Society. Ed. by John Fuegi, Reinhold Grimm, Jost Hermand et al. Vols. 1–3 Frankfurt/Main: Athenäum, 1971–1973. Beginning with Volume 4 (1974) as *Brecht Jahrbuch* in Frankfurt/Main: Suhrkamp, 1975–1981. From 11 (1982) on, *Brecht Yearbook* 14 (1989ff.) Madison: University of Wisconsin Press.

Cook, Bruce. *Brecht in Exile*. New York: Holt, Reinhart & Winston, 1983.

Demetz, Peter (Ed.). *Brecht: A Collection of Critical Essays*. Englewood Cliffs, N.J.: Prentice Hall Inc., 1965.

Dickson, Keith A. "Brecht: An Aristotelian magré lui." *Modern Drama* 11 (1967): 111–121.

———. *Towards Utopia: A Study of Brecht*. Oxford: Clarendon Press, 1978.

Esslin, Martin. *Bertolt Brecht*. New York and London: Columbia University Press, 1969.

———. *Brecht: A Choice of Evils: A Critical Study of the Man, His Work and His Opinions*. London and New York: Methuen, 1984.

———. *Brecht: The Man and His Work*. Garden City: Doubleday and Company, 1961.

Ewen, Frederic. *Bertolt Brecht: His Life, His Art and His Times*. New York: The Citadel Press, 1967.

Fuegi, John. *Brecht & Co.: Sex, Politics and the Making of Modern Drama*. New York: Grove Press, 1994.

———. *The Essential Brecht*. Los Angeles: Hennessey and Ingalls, 1972.

Gray, Ronald. *Brecht*. Edinburgh and London: Oliver and Boyd, 1961.

———. *Brecht the Dramatist*. Cambridge: Cambridge University Press, 1976.

Haas, Willy. *Bert Brecht*. Translated by Max Knight and Joseph Fabry. New York: Frederick Ungar Publishing Company, 1970.

Hayman, Ronald (Ed.). *Contemporary Playwrights: Bertolt Brecht: The Plays*. London: Heinemann, and Totowa, N. J.: Barnes and Noble, 1984.

Hecht, Werner. "The Development of Brecht's Theory of the Epic Theatre, 1918–1933." *Tulane Drama Review* 6 (1961): 40–97.

Kahn, Gordon. *Hollywood on Trial*. Foreword by Thomas Mann. New York: Boni & Gaer, 1948.

Kenney, William. *The Plays of Bertolt Brecht*. New York: Monarch Press, 1965.

Knust, Herbert and Mew Siegfried (Eds.) *Essays on Brecht: Theater and Politics*. Chapel Hill: University of North Carolina Press, 1974.

Lüthy, Herbert. "Of Poor Brecht." *Encounter* 34 (1956): 33–53.

Lyon, James K. *Bertolt Brecht in America*. Princeton: Princeton University Press, 1980.

Lyons, Charles R. *Bertolt Brecht: The Despair and the Polemic*. Carbondale: Southern Illinois University Press, 1968.

Parker, R. B. "Dramaturgy in Shakespeare and Brecht." *University of Toronto Quarterly* 32, 3 (1963): 229–246.

Politzer, Heinz. "How Epic Is Brecht's Epic Theater?" *MLQ* 24 (June 1962): 99–114.

Sagar, Keith M. "Brecht in Neverneverland: *The Caucasian Chalk Circle*." *MD* 9 (1966): 11–17.

Schoeps, Karl H. *Bertolt Brecht*. New York: Frederick Ungar, 1977.

Spalter, Max. *Brecht's Tradition*. Baltimore: Johns Hopkins University Press, 1967.

Speirs, Ronald. *Bertolt Brecht*. London: MacMillan Publishers, 1987.

Thomson, Peter and Glendyr Sacks (Eds.). *The Cambridge Companion to Brecht.* Cambridge: Cambridge University Press, 1994.

Völker, Klaus. *Brecht: A Biography.* Translated by John Nowell. New York: The Seabury Press, 1978.

———. *Brecht Chronicle.* Translated by Fred Wieck. New York: The Seabury Press, 1975.

Weber, Betty N. and Hubert Heinen (Eds.). *Bertolt Brecht: Political Theory and Literary Practice.* Athens: The University of Georgia Press, 1980.

Weideli, Walter. *The Art of Bertolt Brecht.* English version by Daniel Russell. New York: New York University Press, 1963.

Weill, Kurt. "Gestus in Music." *Tulane Drama Review* 6, 1 (1961): 28–32.

Weisstein, Ulrich. "Brecht in America: A Preliminary Survey." *Modern Language Notes* 4 (1963): 373–196.

Willett, John. *The Theatre of Bertolt Brecht: A Study from Eight Aspects.* New York: New Directions, 1968.

Witt, Hubert (Ed.). *Brecht as They Knew Him.* Translated by John Peet. Berlin: Seven Seas Publishers, 1974.

Index of
Themes and Ideas

Bertolt Brecht /
E BERTO

31057001336984